Wild, Wild World of Animals

Birds
of Sea, Shore & Stream

A TIME-LIFE TELEVISION BOOK

Produced in Association with Vineyard Books, Inc.

Editor: Eleanor Graves
Senior Consultant: Lucille Ogle
Text Editor: Richard Oulahan
    Associate Text Editors: Bonnie Johnson, Peter Ainslie, Ivan N. Kaye
    Author: Will Bradbury
    Assistant Editor: Regina Grant Hersey
    Advisory Editor: Bertel Bruun
    Literary Research: Ellen Schachter
    Text Research: Trish Kiesewetter
    Copy Editors: Robert J. Myer, Greg Weed
Picture Editor: Richard O. Pollard
    Picture Research: Judith Greene
    Permissions: Cecilia Waters
Book Designer and Art Director: Jos. Trautwein
Production Coordinator: Jane L. Quinson

WILD, WILD WORLD OF ANIMALS
TELEVISION PROGRAM
Producers: Jonathan Donald and Lothar Wolff
This Time-Life Television Book is published by Time-Life Films, Inc.
Bruce L. Paisner, *President*
J. Nicoll Durrie, *Business Manager*

THE AUTHOR

WILL BRADBURY was a writer for *Life* magazine for 11 years and head of *Life*'s Science Department for three years. He is presently a free-lance writer and is working on his third novel.

THE CONSULTANTS

WILLIAM G. CONWAY, General Director of the New York Zoological Society, is an internationally known zoologist with a special interest in wildlife conservation. He is on the boards of a number of scientific and conservation organizations, including the U. S. Appeal of the World Wildlife Fund and the Cornell Laboratory of Ornithology. He is a past president of the American Association of Zoological Parks and Aquariums.

DR. JAMES W. WADDICK, Curator of Education of the New York Zoological Society, is a herpetologist specializing in amphibians. He has written for many scientific journals and has participated in expeditions to Mexico, Central America and Ecuador. He is a member of the American Society of Ichthyologists and Herpetologists, a Fellow of the American Association of Zoological Parks and Aquariums and a member of its Public Education Committee.

DR. DONALD BRUNING, Curator of Ornithology of the New York Zoological Society and adjunct associate professor of zoology at Fordham University, has written numerous articles on birds. He was a delegate to the International Ornithological Congress and to the International Committee for Bird Preservation in Canberra, Australia, in 1974. He has done extensive research on rheas in Argentina.

JOSEPH L. BELL is Deputy Director of Zoology and Chairman and Curator of the Department of Ornithology of the New York Zoological Society. Mr. Bell has written widely on birds, with an emphasis on their captive management and breeding. He has made several collecting and natural-history tours to Central and South America. Mr. Bell is a Fellow of the American Association of Zoological Parks and Aquariums and a director of the International Wild Waterfowl Association.

Wild, Wild World of Animals

Birds
of Sea, Shore & Stream

Based on the television series
Wild, Wild World of Animals

Published by

TIME-LIFE FILMS

The excerpt from Walden by Henry David Thoreau is used courtesy of Random House, Inc.

The excerpt from "The Rime of the Ancient Mariner," reprinted from The Complete Poetical Works of Samuel Taylor Coleridge, edited by E. H. Coleridge 1912, is used by permission of Oxford University Press.

The excerpt from Flamingo Hunt by Paul A. Zahl, copyright © 1953 by Paul A. Zahl, is used by permission of The Bobbs-Merrill Company, Inc.

The excerpt from King Solomon's Ring by Konrad Z. Lorenz, copyright © 1952 by Konrad Lorenz, translated by Marjorie Kerr Wilson, is used by permission of Thomas Y. Crowell Company, Inc. and Methuen & Co., Ltd.

ISBN 0-913948-07-1

Library of Congress Catalog Card Number: 76-15576

Contents

Introduction
by Will Bradbury

WHAT MAKES BIRDS DIFFERENT FROM OTHER CREATURES? Most people will probably answer: the miracle of flight, that glorious, enviable, seemingly effortless ability birds have for rising from the earth, crossing over great reaches of land and water and then gliding down to more promising areas. Ask an ornithologist or a birdwatcher, though, and they are likely to point to feathers, the single characteristic that distinguishes birds from all other living things. And in fact it was the individual feather, shaped from reptilian scales by evolutionary pressures millions of years ago, that truly made avian flight possible. And it was the widespread application of this marvelous adaptation that brought certain birds into a watery world—sometimes far from land, more often along the coastal shore and even on inland lakes and rivers.

How did that first crucial bit of evolutionary alchemy—the change from scale to feather—come about? Though the span of time involved (anywhere from 150 to 225 million years) is hard to comprehend, the transformation itself is not. It probably began about 200 million years ago, during the Triassic period, when a number of scaly, lizardlike creatures scampered about on their hind legs or climbed into the trees. Forebears of the dinosaurs and their flying cousins, the pterodactyls, these running, climbing creatures gradually developed long, loose scales. In some cases—probably under the winnowing pressures of time and predation—their loose scales even fringed their bodies. The advantage was clear enough: Longer, lighter scales, possibly even split and frayed at the edges, made it easier to glide between branches, to gather food, to escape predators and to maintain body temperature.

The story of how birds evolved could only be surmised until little more than 100 years ago (and less than three years after Darwin's *Origin of Species*), when man got his first real look at the developing prototype in a 150-million-year-old wedge of Bavarian limestone. Called Archaeopteryx—for ancient wing or bird—the limestone fossil showed, with remarkable clarity, the imprint of true feathers. And though they draped the crow-sized body of a small and probably awkward flier, the feathers signaled the dawn of the era of flying birds. They also marked the beginning of other changes in the bodies of those early birds. Ever so gradually spines developed and ribs fused. Bones grew lighter as they became hollow. Where necessary for strength, they were honeycombed with cartilaginous or bony struts. At the same time, the breastbone grew a keel, the anchor point for massive flight muscles, and breathing and digestive systems became streamlined and more efficient. Many of today's birds "chew" with a muscular stomach or gizzard, and food is converted to flight fuel with minimal delay. Eyes, a flying creature's most vital sensors, kept pace, evolving long-range monocular and binocular capacities, the combined size of the organs often being as large as the entire brain. As for reproduction, the eggs of birds were merely an improvement on the more vulnerable eggs of reptiles.

By the Pliocene period, some 12 to 13 million years ago, most design

8

Brandt's cormorants perch on a rock stack in Monterey Bay, California.

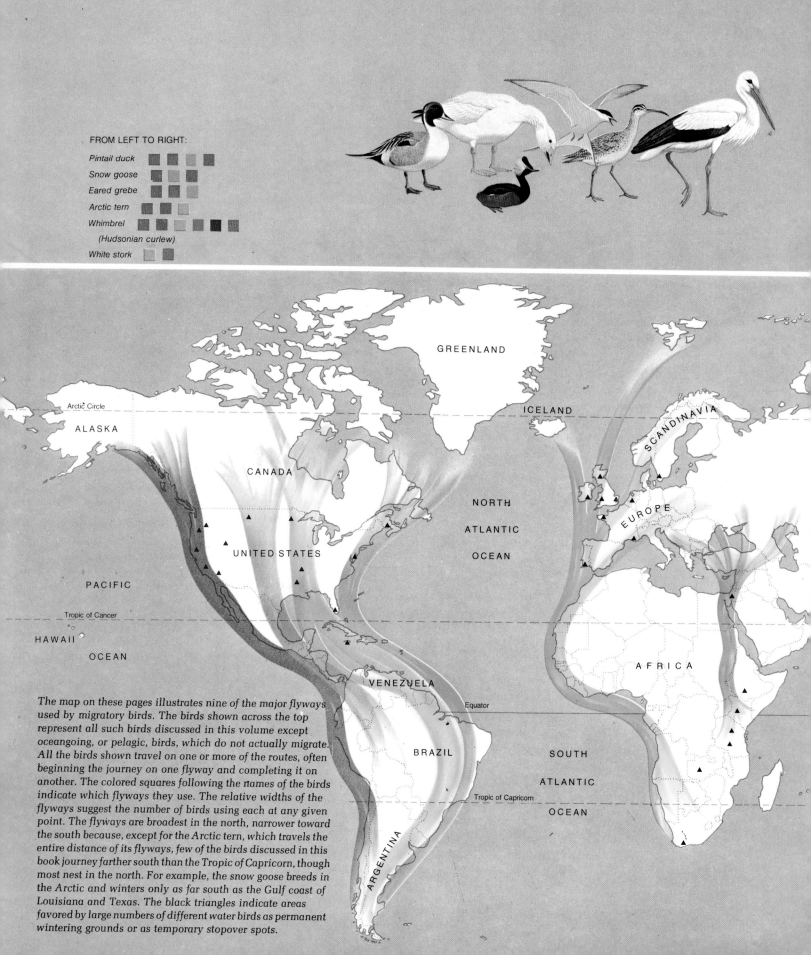

FROM LEFT TO RIGHT:

Pintail duck

Snow goose

Eared grebe

Arctic tern

Whimbrel

(Hudsonian curlew)

White stork

GREENLAND

ICELAND

SCANDINAVIA

Arctic Circle

ALASKA

CANADA

EUROPE

NORTH

ATLANTIC

OCEAN

UNITED STATES

PACIFIC

Tropic of Cancer

HAWAII

OCEAN

AFRICA

VENEZUELA

Equator

BRAZIL

SOUTH

ATLANTIC

Tropic of Capricorn

OCEAN

ARGENTINA

The map on these pages illustrates nine of the major flyways used by migratory birds. The birds shown across the top represent all such birds discussed in this volume except oceangoing, or pelagic, birds, which do not actually migrate. All the birds shown travel on one or more of the routes, often beginning the journey on one flyway and completing it on another. The colored squares following the names of the birds indicate which flyways they use. The relative widths of the flyways suggest the number of birds using each at any given point. The flyways are broadest in the north, narrower toward the south because, except for the Arctic tern, which travels the entire distance of its flyways, few of the birds discussed in this book journey farther south than the Tropic of Capricorn, though most nest in the north. For example, the snow goose breeds in the Arctic and winters only as far south as the Gulf coast of Louisiana and Texas. The black triangles indicate areas favored by large numbers of different water birds as permanent wintering grounds or as temporary stopover spots.

Little egret

Mongolian plover

Least Whimbrel

Bar-headed goose

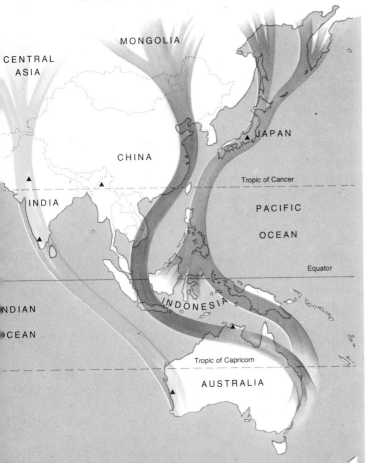

SIBERIA

Arctic Circle

MONGOLIA

CENTRAL ASIA

CHINA

JAPAN

Tropic of Cancer

INDIA

PACIFIC

OCEAN

Equator

INDONESIA

NDIAN

CEAN

Tropic of Capricorn

AUSTRALIA

changes were completed, with three or four fossil species indicating the evolutions of modern genera. By the Pleistocene period, a million or so years ago, a peak was reached when more than 11,000 bird species may have existed. Later, perhaps no more than a half-million years ago, as the cutting edge of the great glaciers sliced across the northern hemisphere, a decline began. Fostered most often by vagaries of climate and predation—and evolutionary dead ending—it has continued ever since. Today, some 9,000 species exist, most ornithologists agree, with perhaps a few yet to be discovered in remote parts of the world. This does not mean that birds as a class (the Latin designation is Aves) are threatened with extinction: There are by the roughest estimate some 100 billion birds living today.

No one can say for sure when the first feathered creature took to the water or why. The process undoubtedly began very early in inland waters and spread slowly, from shore to surf to reef and finally into deep ocean wildernesses. Yet the first evolutionary dilemma such pioneering birds came up against is one that still dominates their ranks—whether it is better, in terms of food and security, to fly above the waves or beneath them. Four orders of the seabirds have developed individual answers to this environmental quandary. The Sphenisciformes, or penguins, through adaptation of feather and wing, have forsaken the skies entirely and have taken totally to the water, continuing to flourish today thanks largely to the extreme harshness and isolation of their surroundings. Their northern, though unrelated, equivalents, the flightless great auks, followed the same evolutionary route and were slaughtered to extinction by predatory, if protein-starved, mariners and whalers.

At the other end of the scale are the Procellariiformes, the albatrosses and their kin, long, narrow-winged, gliding and soaring aerialists capable of surviving for years at sea without touching land except to nest. The Charadriiformes constitute the largest of the orders and include the gulls, plovers, skuas, jaegers, skimmers and the greatest of all migra-

11

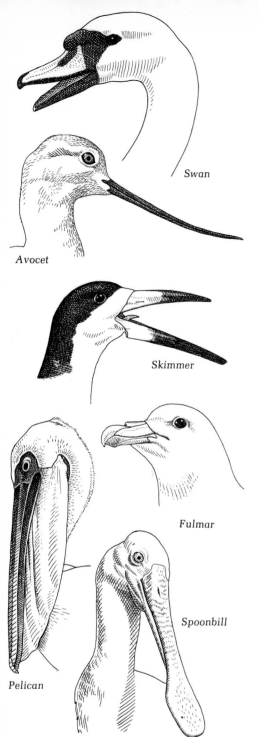

Swan

Avocet

Skimmer

Fulmar

Spoonbill

Pelican

The illustrations above show the different beak structures of various aquatic birds. The swan's rounded bill has toothlike serrations that strain out particles of food; the avocet moves its upturned bill from side to side to dislodge food from muddy marsh bottoms; the skimmer fishes by slicing the surface of the water with its long lower mandible; the fulmar has tube-enclosed nostrils, which aid in the excretion of excess salt; the pelican uses its beak's attached pouch to scoop fish from the water; the spoonbill's long, broad bill sifts through mud for food.

tory animals, the terns. Originally shore feeders, the birds of this order spread out in several directions. Though most continue to mine the riches of the tidal zone, some, like the woodcock, have moved inland permanently, while others have ventured out to sea and a few even shuttle between sea and shore, responding to the seasons. The Pelecaniformes, made up of six families, form the fourth group, an assemblage that varies as much in habitat as in feeding style, ranging from the saltwater, high-diving brown pelican to the submarinelike cormorant and the freshwater darter and white pelican.

In general, shorebirds are defined as those birds that are dependent on water for their food but always return to land after foraging and never wander very far from their rather limited habitat. Seabirds are wide-ranging ocean wanderers that roam over entire hemispheres and come back to land only to breed. There are exceptions to the general definitions, though: Alcids—auks and related species—though shorebirds, behave just like seabirds and must seek land in order to breed.

For all its bounty, however, the sea is an intricate, frequently dangerous and constantly changing food machine, keyed and powered not only by the tides but also by the spin of the earth and dramatic variations in temperature across its surface. As a result, birds of sea and shore as well as their inland cousins have developed an impressive array of tools and weapons in their struggle to survive. As a protective covering feathers are of primary importance to birds, especially in the water, which is often cold, and without their protection survival is unlikely. Penguins have developed thick, short-feathered, foul-weather coverings and, unique among birds, have feathers that grow all over their bodies and not in rows as with other birds; eider ducks exhibit the lightest, yet warmest, down in the world; and bottom-walking dippers waterproof their feathers with secretions from greatly enlarged preen glands. Foot adaptation is equally—and crucially—important in water birds and ranges from the webbed feet of ducks and geese to the spread toes and long nails of birds capable of trotting across lily pads and to the individually flapped toes of grebes. Among the wading shorebirds, the different bills are as remarkable for their diversity as for their efficiency. Even drinking can be a problem for seabirds, especially if only salt water is available. Petrels and certain other saltwater birds have special glands above their eyes that excrete salt from their bodies, enabling them to drink from the briniest seas.

Even with adaptations of feather and bill, sea, shore and certain inland birds must be attuned not just to the location of their prey but to its feeding cycles as well. Most coastal birds feed actively during the day, while those that are truly oceangoing, or pelagic, are also busy at night, when schools of fish rise near the surface. The skimmer, with its curiously extended lower mandible and catlike eyes, is generally found fishing in the evening or early morning in the calm waters of protected bays.

In the evolution of seabirds, the greatest influence has been the change of seasons, which causes the food supply to die off and disappear beneath the ice and has made seabirds the greatest of all migratory creatures and extraordinary colonizers and parents as well. The Arctic tern, unquestionably the champion world traveler, commutes 12,000 miles, almost from pole to pole, twice each year, a distance nearly equal to the circumference of the earth. The golden plover, an impressive second to the Arctic tern, spends the summer months in its natural home—the Arctic tundra—and then heads south for Argentina and surroundings similar to those it left 8,000 miles behind. Distance, though impressive, is just one of migration's mysteries. How a single bird, or even great flocks of birds, can fly thousands of miles across sea and land and locate annual nesting sites with missilelike accuracy is a mystery that ornithologists have never explained. And though homing instincts are the enigmatic inner core of the migration riddle, their unerring accuracy is astonishing. One Manx shearwater, flown by plane across the Atlantic to Boston from an island off the Welsh coast, was home in less than two weeks, and a Laysan albatross, released some 3,200 miles from its home on Sand Island in the Midway atoll, regained its nest in 10 days.

Returning home to habitual nesting areas constitutes the second—and most vital—half of the migration cycle. And it is not surprising that nature has well endowed seabirds for the trip. Because nesting and raising young are vital parts of the life cycle of all birds, it is a serious undertaking for seabirds, which mature slowly, lay only one or two eggs and are often clumsy and vulnerable on land. As with most birds, nesting sites therefore must meet at least two requirements: First, they must provide a readily available supply of food; and, second, they must be safe. Islands or uninhabited coastal regions usually fulfill both requirements and are often selected. And at breeding time these rocky, vertical warrens of seabirds become one of the great marvels of the avian world. The nesting colony is a metropolis of millions of swarming, mating, feeding, infant-tending seabirds—shearwaters on the Tristan da Cunha islands in the South Atlantic, perhaps, or murres in the North Atlantic or guano-producing cormorants beside the anchovy-rich waters off Peru.

Are there other reasons for such intense clustering behavior (in some cases several pairs may nest within a single square yard) in seabirds? Some scientists have suggested that these birds may gather together in such massive congregations in order to reinforce—or even trigger—instinctive drives to mate, hatch and care for their young.

Many seabirds have developed techniques for predigesting food for their young, making it easier for the nestling to eat. Gulls and storks deposit the food directly in front of their young when their digestive systems have developed sufficiently. Spoonbills and pelicans open their mouths so their chicks can feed from them directly. Penguins, trekking hundreds of miles across frozen ice and tundra, provide their young with a kind of fish soup that comes from their crops.

The rise of seabirds and shorebirds from crawling amphibians and reptiles to masters of flight, adapted to a watery world, is emphatic proof that living things possess an infinite capacity to adapt and survive in the face of the most formidable obstacles.

13

Penguins and Puffins

Because they present such a striking caricature of humans, with their snowy shirtfronts, frock coats and comical Chaplinesque waddles, penguins are among the most appealing of all seabirds. Adapted to the harshest climate on earth, they are creatures of freezing seas, ice floes and subzero weather, an environment in which no other bird could survive. Most of them, however, now live in more temperate habitats. Their dense, waterproof feathers cover their entire bodies and resemble the sleek coats of seals more than the plumage of other birds, and under their skin is a layer of fat that serves not only as a suit of thermal underwear but also as a source of food during the breeding season, when they are forced to stay out of the water for long periods.

Creatures of the southern hemisphere, the 17 species of penguins are usually associated with frozen habitats, although some have made their way to the coasts of Africa, South America and Australia, and one species of fewer than 2,000 members, the endangered Galápagos penguin, has followed that great cold-water stream, the Humboldt Current, to the Galápagos Islands, just on the Equator. The emperor, king and Adélie penguins, on the other hand, live out their lives in the Antarctic region. Wherever they live, though, penguins are always dependent on cold-water currents and the rich supply of fish and other marine life they contain.

Curiously, the flightless penguins' closest relatives are from the order that includes those soaring, indefatigable masters of flight, the albatrosses. But even though they lack airborne power and are awkward on land, penguins are incomparable swimmers, the most truly marine birds, rivaling seals and porpoises in their underwater skills. In the evolutionary process their wings have become hardened, flat oars, fused at the elbows, enabling them to streak through water at speeds up to 25 miles per hour, sometimes diving hundreds of feet deep in quest of food and popping up like a cork five or six feet above the water's surface to land on the top of ice floes.

Prodigious migrants, penguins often travel hundreds of miles through frigid seas and over hostile terrain for their annual mating at traditional nesting sites. Naturally monogamous, they nevertheless nest together in huge colonies that may number a million birds or more. Their homing instinct is uncanny: Two Adélie penguins that were released more than 2,000 miles from their normal breeding grounds made their way back across the Antarctic ice in 10 months. Nor are penguins easily put off by intruders in their nesting sites: Every year the little blue penguins of Australia waddle imperturbably across floodlit beaches to their nests while crowds of rubbernecking tourists look on. Once on the nest—usually a shallow, crudely scooped-out hole with a few rocks to serve as windbreakers—the female penguins lay two or three eggs and brood them as other birds do.

The emperor penguin, at four feet the largest of the order, is an extraordinary exception. The only bird that never sets foot on solid land, the emperor lays its single egg directly on the Antarctic ice in the bitterly cold, 24-hour night of midwinter. As soon as the female lays her egg she departs for the sea and food, leaving her mate as custodian of the egg. For 64 days, while polar gales howl and temperatures plummet to 40°F. below zero, the male holds the egg on his feet, protecting it with a fold of fatty skin. Huddled in the cold with hundreds of other males, he regularly takes his turn at the perimeter of the flock, screening off the piercing winds until the egg is finally hatched, just as the polar spring begins and food is most abundant. For a few days the male feeds the hatchling with a milky secretion drawn from his crop, until the mother penguin reappears. Having lost nearly a third of his body weight during the winter vigil, the male is then free to struggle off to the sea and break his long fast.

The scientific name, *Pinguinnus impennis*, formerly designated the great auk, an unrelated but similar-looking bird that was finally hunted to extinction in 1844. Because modern penguins so closely resemble great auks, the explorers who first sighted these birds called them penguins. The surviving relatives of the great auk—the lesser auks, murres and puffins—occupy in northern waters the same niche that penguins fill in the south. With their legs set awkwardly far back, they are as clumsy as penguins on land; but they are strong fliers and excellent swimmers and divers. The largest members of the family Alcidae are the common and thick-billed murres and the razor-billed auks. The puffins, with their gaudy, parrotlike beaks and crested head feathers, are the clowns of the family. Living in a circumpolar habitat throughout the Arctic region, often in colonies of a million or more, the alcids feed mostly on fish and invertebrates, breed in the spring and produce a single egg in crevices or burrows.

14

Nesting Colony

As many as half a million Adélie penguins like those at right may gather in one location in the Antarctic during the annual breeding season. The "ecstatic" greeting display (above) is a part of the ritual that unites Adélie couples, which, like most penguins, remain monogamous throughout their lives. If one mate does not return to the Antarctic breeding site, however, the survivor will take a new partner.

Like the emperor penguins, Adélie males assume responsibility for egg incubation when the females leave to find food, and since he loses some 40 percent of his body weight during this long, foodless vigil, it is important that his bond with the female be strong enough to bring her back at hatching time. Otherwise the emaciated father might have to feed and raise an insatiable chick by himself. Adult Adélies are fiercly possessive of their breeding grounds. Young birds arriving at the grounds for the first time sometimes cause an uproar by unknowingly squatting on an older resident's turf.

While his mate is off searching for food, the king penguin at left on the sub-Antarctic island of South Georgia incubates their egg. The hatching cycle is so exquisitely timed that young penguins will be ready to fend for themselves at precisely the most favorable moment—early December. Then the shore ice begins to melt with the arrival of the Antarctic summer, and marine life becomes abundant. The young, along with their elders, will dive unhesitatingly into the water to pursue the fish, squid and shrimp that make up their diet.

The Rigors of Parenthood

The responsibilities of fatherhood begin early among the penguins. At left, a king penguin incubates his egg by placing it atop his feet and lowering a blubbery fold of skin to cover it. The procedure does away with any need for a nest, frees the king from territorial disputes and insures that the egg will be kept warm even at −40° F. The king penguin's incubation behavior is unusual and is shared only by the emperor. Most penguins build some kind of primitive nest. The Adélies, for example, amass a pile of stones and pebbles. When they feel like enlarging their rocky abode they sneak over to the nest of an absent neighbor and steal his stones. However, emperor and king penguins lay only one egg, which, given their exotic manner of incubation, is understandable. Other penguins produce two and sometimes three eggs. The laying time for the emperor and king is in May or June, when the Antarctic is enveloped in total darkness. The incubation period of 64 days is comparable to the gestation period of many small mammals, including dogs.

18

After hunting at sea, penguin parents return to the nest and regurgitate digested food directly into the ravenous hatchling's mouth (right). Both mother and father participate in this nourishing ritual. In a dignified pose (above), penguin parents and their chick look like nothing so much as a trio of tuxedo-clad humans.

On the March

The parade shown at right is the long procession of the royal penguins as they pass from the sea to their rookery on Macquarie Island, off the coast of Australia. The island is their only home. Royals have sharp claws that latch onto rocks like grappling hooks. As the photograph above and on the cover shows, they also sport impressive crests of long feathers above their eyes. In common with every other species of crested penguins, royals leave their breeding grounds in late summer or fall and spend three to five months at sea. They are believed to follow a northward current, which enables them to spend the whole seaborne period in water of a constant temperature. The male and female share the incubation chores for 33 to 36 days, leaning forward during the entire time in the manner common to other penguins at an awkward 45-degree angle.

20

The Madding Crowd

Nothing exemplifies the gregarious nature of penguins more dramatically than their awesome annual crowd scenes like the one shown at left. Thousands of king penguins assemble on their breeding grounds with no regard at all for the theories of population density which dictate that bloodshed must inevitably accompany such overcrowding. The kings, who exhibit little sense of territoriality, seem to get along amiably, even when packed into a nesting site. In common with other penguins, however, they may become nettled by human visitors who intrude on their breeding grounds. When this happens, their flippers can be used effectively for battering the shins of such curious unfeathered bipeds. Penguin sociability is well documented, but still there are rare moments, such as that shown in the desolate scene below, when a penguin, like the solitary Adélie, wants to be alone.

Penguin Aquacade

Penguins lost the power of flight about 100 million years ago. But they swim well enough to attain speeds of 25 miles an hour. They leap from the water like porpoises (above), using their powerful flippers like wings. Like the Magellan penguin in the filmstrip on the opposite page, penguins glide through the water, feeding just under the surface. They are so much at home in water that they do not, in fact, know how to eat on land. Zookeepers have found it necessary to force-feed captive penguins for weeks before they learn to pick up the fish thrown to them. When they travel on land (below) penguins waddle awkwardly. Emperor penguins have a more functional mode of locomotion (opposite). They flop on their ample bellies and propel themselves across the ice like sleds, using their flippers as paddles. The feet serve as pistonlike boosters, helping the penguins to move faster than a man can ski.

Puffin Profile

Native to northern regions such as Greenland and Spitzbergen, common puffins (above) migrate to the coasts of New England and Europe in the winter. Mating takes place when they return to the North Atlantic in the spring. Puffins nest in burrows at the end of serpentine tunnels, which they find or dig in cliffs or hillsides (opposite, right) near the ocean. They lay a single, roundish, white egg and when it hatches, the lone chick is well fed by its parents. Expert fishers (left), they provide the chick with its own weight every day in fish, mussels and sea urchins, so that after six weeks the chick is heavier than its parents. They depart soon afterward, leaving their overstuffed offspring to find its way to the seashore, with the extra weight providing sustenance for the first days on its own, while it learns for itself the art of fishing and flying.

Because its wings are very short in relation to the size of its body, a puffin in flight (above) represents a triumph of willpower over physical shortcomings. In the absence of a stiff wind, these portly birds often splash along for some distance to get airborne. Then, their propulsion is rapid, but they work terribly hard, flapping wings violently to remain aloft.

The puffins at right are out for a stroll on a grassy cliffside on the island of Røst, off the Norwegian coast. Occasionally one of the puffins will break from the dignified perambulation and plunge off the cliff, looping over in the air and back up onto the nesting site, repeating the clownish maneuver over and over.

In the Wake of the Great Auk

What the penguin is to the southern hemisphere the auk is to the northern. But there is one significant difference: Auks can fly. Not that they fly very well, however. Their wings flap overtime to get them up to a speed of 30 miles per hour. But when the auk dives into the water in search of a meal, it enters its element. The bird literally "flies" under the surface, its strong, short wings propelling it through the water. The two modern auks shown above, the parakeet auklets (left) and the British razorbill (right), are both relatives of the great auk, the last of whose number perished at the hand of man on Eldey Island off the Icelandic coast in 1844. The razorbill can be seen bobbing along the surface of the water like a cork, then diving nimbly for fish. During the breeding season European auks gather on cliffs above the sea (opposite), where the brooding mothers lay one egg in a rock crevice, making no effort to build a nest. Since the egg is pyriform, or pear-shaped, it will spin in the wind but will not roll off the cliff. In common with many another bird, the auks are frequent victims of oil pollution, falling like their fabled ancestor to the ravages of man.

28

European auks gather on Bjornoya Bird Mountain in Norway (left). The chicks of cliff-nesting auks leave their ledges within two weeks of hatching. This behavior is a sharp contrast to that of the auklets, which are hatched in burrows and huddle in the safety of their little bunkers for two months before venturing out into the world. The auk family ranges around the Arctic Ocean, with the heaviest concentrations in the Bering Sea.

29

Pelecaniformes

Comical and ungainly on the ground, the brown pelican becomes a creature of consummate grace and beauty when it takes to the air. In V-formation echelons, the big birds are in their element when they are airborne, winging steadily along with slow, powerful strokes (about 1.3 per second, compared with the frantic 50 to 60 flutters of some hummingbirds). The rhythm of the lead bird's flight undulates back along the string as each trailing bird picks it up in unison. The brown pelicans often fly in formation when they are hunting, and when the moment to strike comes, they undergo another breathtaking transformation. Plummeting downwind into the sea from a height of 10 to 30 feet, they drop with wings half closed, their great throat (or gular) pouches gaping to scoop up their prey, and crash like torpedoes into the sea. Moments later they bob to the surface, buoyed by hundreds of subcutaneous air sacs in their squat bodies, and spill out as much as a gallon or more of excess water from their bulging gular pouches before gobbling their catch of fish.

The brown pelican, a native of the Americas, is the only high diver in the family. The other six species hunt together in shallow water, forming semicircles and dipping their bills like fishnets until they flush and trap the fish they have rounded up in their yawning pouches. Occasionally they will beat the water with their wings in order to corral the fish. Although pelicans are extremely sociable, flocking together in great numbers to breed and hunt, some young, sexually immature birds and an occasional adult stray away from the group and become loners. Pelicans are found in coastal waters and sometimes far inland on every continent except Antarctica.

Other members of the order Pelecaniformes are lone fishers, with individual techniques of pursuing their quarry. The freshwater anhinga, or darter, which fishes inland streams, actually spears its prey with its stiletto bill and then flings it in the air and adroitly catches it head first as it falls. Occasionally, an anhinga will vary the routine by scraping its bill against a rock or tree to remove its catch. Anhingas have the disconcerting habit of deflating the air sacs that make their bodies float and swimming half submerged with only their snakelike necks and heads projecting above the surface. This has understandably given rise to tales of sea serpents and labeled the anhinga with its other common name, the snakebird.

The cormorants, underwater fishers *par excellence*, will dive as deep as 30 feet in pursuit of a fish or a squid. A cormorant carefully positions its quarry before eating it so that the scales will not catch in its throat. In Japan and other parts of the Orient, caged cormorants are used as aids to fishermen, going to sea with hemp choke-collars around their necks to prevent them from eating the fish they catch. One of the 30 species in the family, the guano cormorant of the Peruvian coast has been called the world's most valuable bird because of the enormous amounts of guano, a phosphate-rich manure, it produces. The guano, a valuable fertilizer, results from the birds' anchovy-rich diet and is widely used in agriculture. Commercial harvesters of guano have provided the birds with large wooden roosting platforms and have sealed off peninsulas where they nest to keep predators away.

The remaining Pelecaniformes—gannets and boobies, tropic-birds and frigate birds—often feed far out at sea. Though they share some characteristics of the rest of the order, such as totipalmate (four-toed webbed) feet, each is basically different from the others. Gannets and their tropical cousins, boobies, are high divers that outclass even the brown pelican when it comes to spectacular free falls. Swooping or plummeting directly into the ocean from heights of as much as 100 feet, they fish in flocks, dropping like a hail of lead pellets when they spot a school of fish and seizing their prey with sharp, scissorlike beaks.

The tropic-bird, or bosunbird—so called for its shrill, high-pitched call that sounds like a bosun's pipe—is the most beautiful of the Pelecaniformes. A graceful, soaring flier and a solitary hunter, the adult is easily recognized by its long streamer tail feathers. The greatest aerialist among the seabirds is the frigate, or man-o'-war, bird. With a hearty appetite for fish, mollusks, baby turtles and jellyfish, the fork-tailed frigate birds snatch flying fishes in midair and aggressively go after the food of other birds, attacking and intimidating gulls, terns, boobies and even pelicans, menacing them with their hooked bills and snatching their food when it drops. It is an unusual fact that a frigate bird will sometimes perch on the upper bill of a feeding pelican when it bobs to the surface, audaciously take fish from the gular pouch as the pelican spills out its load of seawater and then wheel off into the wind, leaving the puzzled pelican to wonder what happened to its dinner.

30

American white pelican

A Remarkable Pouch

The unique webbing of all four toes sets the members of the order Pelecaniformes apart from other water birds, and the distensible gular pouch of the true pelicans, such as the European white pelican (above) and the brown pelican (opposite), readily distinguishes them from their relatives, the boobies, gannets, cormorants, tropic-birds, frigate birds and anhingas. This sac of skin hangs between the flexible bones of the birds' lower mandible, while the upper mandible serves as nothing more than a lid. Al-

though the pouch can hold as much as three gallons, it cannot, as popular myth has it, "hold enough food for a week." In fact, the gular sac is not used for storage at all but functions as a net that scoops up fish from the water. Whether it feeds by cooperative fishing or, like the brown pelican, by plunge-diving, once a pelican has made a catch it opens its mouth and tilts its head to the side to spill out the water. If, at this point, the fish is not plucked right out of the pelican's mouth by a wily gull or tern, it is swallowed.

Heads drawn back between their shoulders, beaks pointed straight toward the sea, the two brown pelicans above zero in on their next meal. Smallest of the seven species of pelicans, the four-foot-long brown pelicans are among the most skillful of diving birds. When they dive, these birds hit the water with tremendous impact, forcing geysers of water high into the air behind them. They dive only a few feet below the water, however, and come to the surface almost immediately. The brown pelican at right, its gular pouch stretched to its limit, engulfs a fish that has been thrown to it. Adult brown pelicans consume an average of between two and three pounds of fish a day, skimmed from the waters off southern North America, Central and South America and the West Indies.

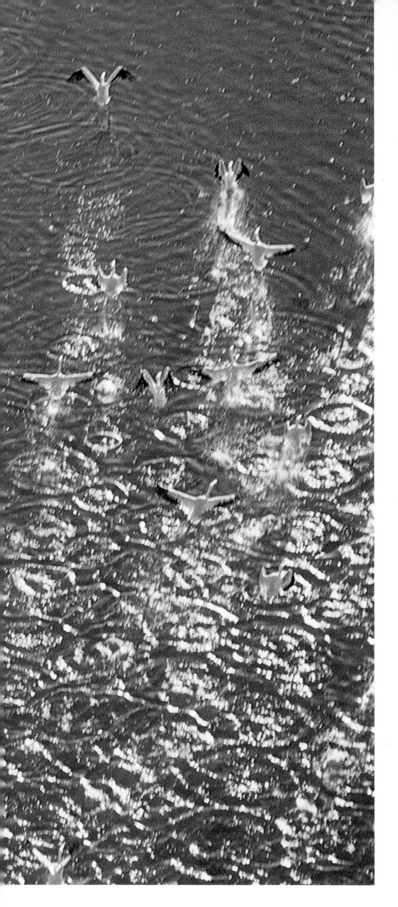

Except for an occasional loner, such as the brown pelican (above), pelicans usually congregate in flocks of up to 50 birds for flying, breeding and feeding. After filling up on fish, the American white pelicans at left take off en masse and head back to their roosting grounds to care for their young.

The red-footed booby (right) is the smallest of all the boobies. It is one of the two tree-nesting species, and, because of the relative inaccessibility and security of its nest, the female lays only one egg. Other ground-nesting boobies are more vulnerable to predators and lay several eggs as a natural insurance that a few chicks will live and the species will survive. The red-footed booby is found on many islands in the Caribbean Sea and the South Atlantic, Indian and Pacific oceans. A huge colony of 140,000 pairs of red-footed boobies resides on Tower Island in the Galápagos Islands, off the coast of Ecuador.

The blue-footed booby (above), at 34 inches long, is the largest of its clan. Its relatively big, webbed feet range in color from light blue to aquamarine. The nesting grounds of the blue-footed booby are scattered over coastal islands from southern Mexico to Ecuador and Peru. Blue-footed boobies lay two and sometimes three eggs, which are incubated by both parents, who then feed their hatchlings for an additional 20 weeks with regurgitated fish. Despite this care only one chick regularly survives to become a fledgling.

Boobies and Gannets

The gannets and boobies are closely related, large-bodied seabirds that, like their cousins, the brown pelicans, plunge-dive for their food. The main difference between the two genera is one of habitat: The gannets inhabit the world's temperate oceans, while the somewhat smaller boobies are found only in warmer, tropical waters. Boobies are very sociable and live in large, sprawling colonies. Gannets also breed in densely populated communities, often made up of thousands of nesting couples, each occupying an area no more than one yard square, an area they heatedly defend—using their long, sharp bills—against intruders. Such close quarters are beneficial, because the greater the number of birds, the better able they are to defend their young from predators. The largest known gannet colony is on the island of St. Kilda off the west coast of Scotland, where some 52,000 birds almost obscure the rugged cliffs.

The masked booby (below), also—and less appropriately—called the blue-faced booby, is an inhabitant of islands in the South Atlantic, South Pacific and Indian oceans. It is often seen far from land following schools of flying fish, its primary food. As with other birds that live near the Equator, masked boobies have no regular breeding season and lay their eggs all year long. Usually two eggs are laid, one of which hatches much later than the other. The firstborn chick rules the roost, making the survival of the younger, smaller nestmate a rare occurrence.

The two northern gannets (above), their necks outstretched and their long beaks crossed in midair, are going through part of the elaborate greeting ceremony common to all mating gannets. It is thought that this complex display of loyalty keeps the bond between a breeding couple strong enough to last the entire 42-day incubation period, when the male and female alternate on the nest. After the single egg is hatched the parents spend an additional 10 to 12 weeks caring for the chick, which is then old enough to start fending for itself.

Cormorants and Anhingas

Members of the family of cormorants, such as the flightless cormorant (opposite) of the Galápagos Islands, are found along almost all the world's coastlines. Anhingas, on the other hand such as the American anhinga (left and below), are inhabitants of inland lakes and rivers. The two families are similar, however, in that both have dense, heavy bones. In addition, they have fewer of the subcutaneous air sacs that give the other members of their Pelecaniformes order their corklike buoyancy. As a result, anhingas and cormorants float low in the water. Feathers that are not waterproof is another characteristic these birds share, so they rarely rest in the water but come on land as soon as they have finished feeding. Once on shore, anhingas and cormorants relax with their wings half extended, drying them in the wind and sun, a ritual that is often preceded by squabbling over the best perching sites.

An American anhinga (right), or water turkey, as it is commonly called in the southern United States, raises high its most recent catch, proof that it is a first-class spear fisherman. Once it solves the problem of getting the fish off its bill and into its mouth—a feat usually accomplished by flipping the fish up in the air and catching it in its bill—the anhinga returns to land (above) to dry off its soaked plumage.

38

Although most cormorants are powerful, though hard-working, fliers, one—the flightless cormorant, seen drying its shrunken wings at left—has lost this capacity altogether. Because it has lived for millions of years on two of the remote Galápagos Islands—Isabela and Fernandina and the waters around them—where it has adequate food and nesting material and no natural enemies, the flightless cormorant had no need to fly and ultimately became completely earthbound. The flightless cormorant is a strong swimmer, keeping its small wings close to its sides and relying instead on its fully webbed feet for propulsion.

Artful Aviators

Inflating its bright red gular sac, a frigate bird (above) soars through the air on wings that have a seven-foot span in flight and are supported by a body that weighs only three pounds. This remarkable anatomical ratio enables the frigate bird to perform spectacular aerial feats and allows it to wheel about for hours searching for food. Although they spend most of their time above the water, frigate birds rarely go into it. Their plumage is only slightly oiled and quickly becomes wet, and their small feet are only partially webbed and are not very effective propellers. Frigate birds are coastal fliers, and the sight of one is a signal to mariners that land is nearby. In contrast, tropic-birds, such as the white-tailed tropic-birds at right, are almost exclusively pelagic. Like most birds that feed on the open sea, tropic-birds are poorly suited for life on land. Their short legs can barely support their weight and make getting aloft a problem. As a result, tropic-birds roost on windswept headlands, giving them a boost in taking off into the air.

Loons and Grebes

The blood-chilling cry is unforgettable: a wailing lament that trails off into maniacal laughter. It proclaims the presence of a loon, and it also explains the bird's reputation as the epitome of insanity ("crazy as a loon"). Actually, loons are canny birds, skilled divers that are so fast in the water that hunters claim half seriously that they are able to dodge their bullets. The ancestors of the loon probably can be traced to a six-foot monster, *Hesperornis regalis*, a fishing bird that inhabited the waters of North America 100 million years ago. According to fossil evidence in Ice Age rocks, modern loons probably evolved some 50 million years ago. They are the only birds whose legs are sunk in their bodies down to the ankle joint. They are also among the few flying creatures that have solid bones, making their specific gravity remarkably close to that of water. Merely by expelling air from their bodies and from under their feathers, they are able to sink below the water's surface with hardly a ripple. With other waterfowl they share a capacity to store extra oxygen in the blood and an inborn resistance, which human divers lack, to the toxicity of excess carbon dioxide. On land, though, these relatively large (five to nine pounds), torpedo-shaped and nearly tailless birds are barely able to get around, a handicap that accounts for their waterside nests and their ability to submerge instantly at the slightest sign of danger. In the air, loons are quite competent fliers, even though they have less wing surface in proportion to body mass than any other bird and require help from the wind in order to make a long, water-splattering takeoff. Once aloft, though, they are strong fliers, beating the air rapidly with their short wings and sometimes reaching speeds of 60 miles per hour. In and under the water they are remarkable swimmers and divers. Powered by their strong, webbed feet, using their wings for balance in turns, they are capable of reaching depths of several hundred feet and, if threatened, of staying submerged for two or three minutes. One bird was recorded as having submerged for 15 minutes. Normally, loons come to land only to nest or to escape storms, even sleeping in the water when they are not breeding. Their two eggs are laid in primitive nests by the water, and the fluffy blackish chicks are hatched after about 30 days. The chicks soon take to the water and often ride on their parents' backs while they learn to swim and dive.

Grebes are sleek water birds that share many of the same traits and skills as loons, though they are not closely related. They, too, are superb divers, capable of instant submersion, and they also ferry their young on their backs. While they do not swim as swiftly or dive as deeply as loons, they are quick and agile enough in the water to earn them the common names of "water witch" and "hell diver." In other ways—the webbing on their feet, their nesting and mating habits, their peculiar predilection for eating their own feathers—grebes are quite different. Their toes, instead of being cross-webbed from toe to toe like a duck's or a loon's, are equipped with finlike lobes. During the mating season male and female grebes perform some bizarre rites of courtship, including one *pas de deux* in which they seem to dance on the water's surface. Their nests, built of vegetation, float on the water, though anchored to a stem or branch, and as the nests rot they provide warmth to help incubate the eggs. There is no substantiated explanation why grebes consume feathers, which form balls in their stomachs, though they may serve to protect internal organs from fish bones.

Rails and their relatives—gallinules, coots and finfoots—are the most varied and widespread of yet another order, Gruiformes, distributed in temperate and tropical climates throughout the world. Long-legged, running, wading or swimming birds of small to medium size, they are creatures that inhabit marsh, pond, lake and plains. Coots and finfoots have lobate webbing on each toe, like that of the grebe; otherwise, the rail family has only its usually damp environment in common with grebes and loons. They are, for the most part, drably colored, elusive birds. The finfoots, inhabitants of jungle rivers in Africa, Southeast Asia and Central and South America, are distinguished by brightly colored scarlet or yellow beaks. In flight they carry their young in special pouches on their backs. When threatened or disturbed, finfoots take refuge in the forest underbrush.

The rare horned coots, denizens of mountain lakes high in the Chilean Andes, have unique nest-building techniques. A breeding pair of birds builds an offshore island of pebbles, anchored to a "basement" and painstakingly constructed of pebbles piled on the lake bottom and topped off, at the water's surface, with a nest of water plants. The nests are built at a distance of about 100 feet from the lakeshore to protect the eggs and chicks from predatory foxes, and they often tower as much as 30 feet from the bottom. Other members of the rail family, notably the crakes, build bowers, or roofed nests, of grass in the dense foliage of their marsh or grassland habitat.

Common loon

Nuptial Plumage

During the cold winter months the four species of loons are covered with dull gray feathers. In March and early April, just before their annual migration north to the Arctic, they undergo a partial molt, losing some feathers in preparation for the growth of their smartly colored, distinctively patterned nuptial plumage. In late May and June, after migration and breeding, loons go through a complete molt, for a brief time losing their wing feathers and rendering them unable to fly. The common loon, gathering twigs for its waterside nest (above), has a shiny greenish-black head and neck and a bold black-and-white design of dots and dashes across its back and tail. Like all members of the family, the common loon never strays far from water, for, as agile and adept as they are at swimming and diving, loons are clumsy and awkward when they move about on land. For this reason, loons always build a slipway from their nests into the water, affording them a quick and easy escape route if predatory enemies approach.

44

Courtship Display

So fully adapted to an aquatic life are the 18 species of grebes that most are, at best, only weak fliers, while some have lost the ability to fly almost completely. Their tails are virtually nonexistent, and their wings are short. In spite of this, some northern species, such as the eared grebe (right), seen perched on its floating nest, make long overland migrations, flying with rapid, labored wingbeats. Like the loons, grebes become distinctively marked during the breeding season, and some, such as the great crested grebes (below), develop bright nuptial plumes around their heads, which they display during their spectacular aquatic courtship dances. With their necks outstretched, the mating couple speeds toward each other. When they are a few inches apart they pull up in a penguinlike posture in order to present premating gifts of weeds or algae.

WALDEN

by Henry David Thoreau

In 1845 Thoreau turned his back on civilization to live for two years in a small hut on the shore of Walden Pond, near Concord, Massachusetts. His account of those wilderness years, Walden, became an American classic. In a chapter entitled "Brute Neighbors," the philosopher-naturalist describes the reaction of a resourceful loon to human intruders.

In the fall the loon (*Colymbus glacialis*) came, as usual, to moult and bathe in the pond, making the woods ring with his wild laughter before I had risen. At rumor of his arrival all the Mill-dam sportsmen are on the alert, in gigs and on foot, two by two and three by three, with patent rifles and conical balls and spy-glasses. They come rustling through the woods like autumn leaves, at least ten men to one loon. Some station themselves on this side of the pond, some on that, for the poor bird cannot be omnipresent; if he dives here he must come up there. But now the kind October wind rises, rustling the leaves and rippling the surface of the water, so that no loon can be heard or seen, though his foes sweep the pond with spy-glasses, and make the woods resound with their discharges. The waves generously rise and dash angrily, taking sides with all water-fowl, and our sportsmen must beat a retreat to town and shop and unfinished jobs. But they were too often successful. When I went to get a pail of water early in the morning I frequently saw this stately bird sailing out of my cove within a few rods. If I endeavored to overtake him in a boat, in order to see how he would manoeuvre, he would dive and be completely lost, so that I did not discover him again, sometimes, till the latter part of the day. But I was more than a match for him on the surface. He commonly went off in a rain.

As I was paddling along the north shore one very calm afternoon, for such days especially they settle on to the lakes, like the milkweed down, having looked in vain over the pond for a loon, suddenly one, sailing out from the shore toward the middle a few rods in front of me, set up his wild laugh and betrayed himself. I pursued with a paddle and he dived, but when he came up I was nearer than before. He dived again, but I miscalculated the direction he would take, and we were fifty rods apart when he came to the surface this time, for I had helped to widen the interval; and again he laughed long and loud, and with more reason than before. He manoeuvred so cunningly that I could not get within half a dozen rods of him. Each time, when he came to the surface, turning his head this way and that, he coolly surveyed the water and the land, and apparently chose his course so that he might come up where there was the widest expanse of water and at the greatest distance from the boat. It was surprising how

quickly he made up his mind and put his resolve into execution. He led me at once to the widest part of the pond, and could not be driven from it. While he was thinking one thing in his brain, I was endeavoring to divine his thought in mine. It was a pretty game, played on the smooth surface of the pond, a man against a loon. Suddenly your adversary's checker disappears beneath the board, and the problem is to place yours nearest to where his will appear again. Sometimes he would come up unexpectedly on the opposite side of me, having apparently passed directly under the boat. So long-winded was he and so unwearlable, that when he had swum farthest he would immediately plunge again, nevertheless; and then no wit could divine where in the deep pond, beneath the smooth surface, he might be speeding his way like a fish, for he had time and ability to visit the bottom of the pond in its deepest part. It is said that loons have been caught in the New York lakes eighty feet beneath the surface, with hooks set for trout,—though Walden is deeper than that. How surprised must the fishes be to see this ungainly visitor from another sphere speeding his way amid their schools! Yet he appeared to know his course as surely under water as on the surface, and swam much faster there. Once or twice I saw a ripple where he approached the surface, just put his head out to reconnoitre, and instantly dived again. I found that it was as well for me to rest on my oars and wait his reappearing as to endeavor to calculate where he would rise; for again and again, when I was straining my eyes over the surface one way, I would suddenly be startled by his unearthly laugh behind me. But why, after displaying so much cunning, did he invariably betray himself the moment he came up by that loud laugh? Did not his white breast enough betray him? He was indeed a silly loon, I thought. I could commonly hear the plash of the water when he came up, and so also detected him. But after an hour he seemed as fresh as ever, dived as willingly, and swam yet farther than at first. It was surprising to see how serenely he sailed off with unruffled breast when he came to the surface, doing all the work with his webbed feet beneath. His usual note was this demoniac laughter, yet somewhat like that of a water-fowl; but occasionally, when he had balked me most successfully and come up a long way off, he uttered a long-drawn unearthly howl, probably more like that of a wolf than any bird; as when a beast puts his muzzle to the ground and deliberately howls. This was his looning,—perhaps the wildest sound that is ever heard here, making the woods ring far and wide. I concluded that he laughed in derision of my efforts, confident of his own resources. Though the sky was by this time overcast, the pond was so smooth that I could see where he broke the surface when I did not hear him. His white breast, the stillness of the air, and the smoothness of the water were all against him. At length, having come up fifty rods off, he uttered one of those prolonged howls, as if calling on the god of loons to aid him, and immediately there came a wind from the east and rippled the surface, and filled the whole air with misty rain, and I was impressed as if it were the prayer of the loon answered, and his god was angry with me; and so I left him disappearing far away on the tumultuous surface.

Rails, Coots and Gallinules

The family of rails is a large (132 species), far-ranging group that includes the true rails, the coots and the gallinules. All are inhabitants of marshes, lakes or ponds. Some, like the Chilean horned coots (above), spend all of their time in the open waters of fresh or brackish lakes. The great majority, however, including the strikingly colored purple gallinule of North and South America (opposite, left) and the richly plumed king rail of eastern North America (opposite, right), are secretive, nocturnal birds whose compressed bodies permit them to hide and feed easily among the reeds of their marshy homes. All rails are members of the order Gruiformes, which, in historic times, has lost more members than any other major order of birds. This is due at least partly to the fact that some rails, until recently, lived virtually without enemies in isolated habitats, and a few species lost the power of flight. With the arrival of man and other predators, they were quickly exterminated. Although many rails are capable of long migrations, others with diminished flying skills take to the air only as a last resort, running from danger rather than flying from it—an infinitely less efficient manner of escape.

Rails, coots and gallinules are omnivorous and able to sustain themselves on a wide variety of plant and animal matter, a trait that accounts for their presence in almost every corner of the globe. The purple gallinule (below) and the king rail (right) are typical of their genera in that they feed mostly on wetlands, their long toes facilitating their movement over the soft marsh mud. The coots, such as the horned coots (opposite), named for the fringed, fleshy protuberance, or "horn," on their foreheads, have flattened, finlike lobes on each toe that are effective swimming and diving aids. Coots thus have a choice of dining areas. In addition to eating on land, they also dive into the water to feed on the rich vegetation growing on the lake's muddy bottom.

49

Albatrosses

With a wingspan of nearly 12 feet—the greatest of any modern flying creature—the wandering albatross is a mariner of the skies without peer. Capable of cruising currents of turbulent ocean air for hours at a time, with barely a flick of its immense wings, skilled at riding out roaring sea gales, the albatross has aroused the awe and envy of sailors. Yet for all their soaring skills, albatrosses are actually rather poor fliers. If the wind dies suddenly, they are forced into a kind of labored flapping flight; and in a calm sea, they are virtually incapable of leaving the water at all. For this reason, most albatrosses are restricted in their range to the southern hemisphere, where, with little land mass to block them, the ocean winds roar unhindered around the globe, churning up deep blue-water rollers— exactly the kind of turbulence the albatrosses and their cousins, the shearwaters and petrels, ride so expertly. Nor are albatrosses likely to migrate northward, barring major changes in wind or weather patterns, because the doldrums—those areas of tropic calm that divide the Atlantic and Pacific oceans on either side of the Equator— form a virtually impassable barrier for the soaring birds, especially in Atlantic waters. In the Pacific, however, three of the family's 13 species have moved north, one nesting on the island of Toroshima, south of Japan, and two in Hawaii's Leeward chain. Yet at breeding time these northern pioneers respond to the tug of ancestral instinct and fly south to mate when southern species do, even though for them it is midwinter.

In direct confrontation with man, albatrosses have been treated with less than reverence. In addition to their proper name, which derives from the Portuguese word *alcatraz*, meaning large pelican, they have also been given such uncomplimentary names as gooney and mollymawk or mollyhawk, which comes from the Dutch word *mollemoks* for "stupid gull." And in some instances albatrosses appear to be exactly that, as when they permit sailors to hook them out of the air on baited lines trailed from moving vessels. The birds' most infamous confrontation with man occurred at the U. S. naval airbase on Midway Island in the Pacific during World War II. The huge flocks of nesting Laysan albatrosses there caused thousands of collisions with naval aircraft, the majority resulting in damage only to the birds. The stubborn birds resisted all efforts to oust them, including exploding rockets and flares and the release of anti-bird chemicals. Finally, on the advice of ornithologists, the military hit on a compromise that proved to be beneficial to both sides: The dunes around the runways were leveled, reducing updrafts and making the airstrips safer for planes and less desirable for nesting birds. Today the albatrosses and airplanes coexist peacefully, each in its own sector of the island.

Members of the Procellariiformes, an order of birds characterized by the plated construction of their bills and the tubelike structure of their nostrils, albatrosses, as a rule, come to land only to breed and some young birds may spend the first two years or more of their life at sea before returning to nest. They land on the water at intervals, though, and are not perpetual fliers. Elaborate courtship rituals, including bill-snapping and wing-flapping gyrations, precede the laying of a single white egg on a volcano-shaped nest. From 60 to 80 days later, usually in March, the chicks hatch and for the next 10 or 11 weeks exist on a diet of regurgitated fish.

Other Procellariiformes are the shearwaters, storm petrels and diving petrels. The order constitutes a remarkable range of sizes, from the 17-pound wandering albatross to the tiny, flyweight storm petrel, weighing only a few ounces. All shearwaters, including fulmars, gadfly petrels and prions, are long-winged, pelagic—oceangoing— birds, and all are communal feeders and colonial breeders. Many nest underground or in crevices and are active only at night. At such times the shrill, eerie sound of nesting shearwaters may have given rise to sailors' tales of haunted islands.

Small, dainty birds with long legs, the storm petrels are erratic and appear almost mothlike in their fluttering flight. One species, Wilson's, is probably the most numerous of all seabirds. With their legs extended and feet paddling rapidly just under the surface, the birds appear to be walking on water as they feed, a trait that inspired early sailors to name them petrel, after St. Peter.

Though their beak and nostril construction is characteristic of the family, the stubby, short-necked diving petrels more closely resemble the unrelated little auks of the northern hemisphere both in appearance and performance. Found exclusively in the south, they fly with rapid, whirring wing strokes, staying, for the most part, close to their colonies. Yet once in sight of their prey, they perform like no other member of their order. Diving headlong into the waves, they "fly" underwater after small crustaceans and fish and then, without altering their stroke for a moment, wing back up into the air again.

Royal albatross

Biennial Mates

The mating behavior of the albatross involves an elaborate greeting ceremony that is among the most fascinating in all the bird kingdom. In the photographs below a pair of waved albatrosses—found only on the Galápagos island of Española—performs the ritual. It usually begins with the birds making deep and graceful bows to each other (top row, left), after which they fence with their tube-nosed beaks (top row, right). A key aspect of the ceremony follows, with the birds raising their heads (bottom row, left) and uttering a prolonged nasal groan, something that sounds like "Ah-h-h," with what one observer describes as "a rapidly rising inflection and a bovine quality." The female finally rotates to face the male (bottom row, right), who steps sideways around her. She appears to demonstrate some affection, yet does not allow him to copulate frequently. After the egg has been laid, the female refuses copulation altogether. The male seems to sublimate his unsatisfied sexual desire by becoming strongly possessive toward the egg, even in some cases reaching the point of expelling his mate forcibly from the nest. The mating ceremony serves to renew the bond between the mating pair. But the bearing and nurture of a single chick takes so long that an albatross couple mates only in alternate years rather than annually.

The black-browed albatrosses (above) inhabit a nesting ground on the Falkland Islands at the tip of South America. Their nests are concave mounds of mud or soil that they line with feathers and grasses. The mound serves as a useful shield, insulating the egg against bad weather. Both parents take a turn at incubating. The newly hatched young are sustained at first by a clear yellow stomach oil, composed of liquefied fat and vitamin A that is secreted by the parents. The strong-smelling liquid can also be discharged from the mouth and tubular nostrils by the adult when it is disturbed. Albatrosses, and all of their cousins with similarly constructed bills, share a powerful, musky body odor so strong that it lingers on for decades, even in museum specimens.

Indefatigable Flier

Since the first Portuguese mariners ventured into the southern oceans, albatrosses have been an inspiring part of life at sea, often convoying vessels for days, even weeks at a time, riding the wind in graceful, tireless, soaring flight. Master of the wind, a Laysan albatross (left) is a lesson in aerodynamics as it glides effortlessly across the Pacific sky. Close up, an albatross presents a stern and menacing visage (below), belying the essentially sociable nature of the big birds, which gather together in huge colonies each year to nest in their remote island rookeries.

The RIME of the ANCIENT MARINER

by Samuel Taylor Coleridge

In Coleridge's famous poem, a ship, driven off course, sails into the region of the South Pole, where it is joined by a large albatross. The crew regards it as a good omen, but suddenly a sailor shoots the bird. There follows a series of dreadful trials, which the mariner's shipmates attribute to the wanton killing. The excerpt describes the beginning of the ancient mariner's woes.

The land of ice, and of fearful sounds where no living thing was to be seen.

[']And through the drifts the snowy clifts
Did send a dismal sheen:
Nor shapes of men nor beasts we ken—
The ice was all between.

The ice was here, the ice was there,
The ice was all around:
It cracked and growled, and roared and
        howled,
Like noises in a swound!

Till a great sea-bird, called the Albatross, came through the snow-fog, and was received with great joy and hospitality.

At length did cross an Albatross,
Through the fog it came;
As if it had been a Christian soul,
We hailed it in God's name.

It ate the food it ne'er had eat,
And round and round it flew.
The ice did split with a thunder-fit;
The helmsman steered us through!

And lo! the Albatross proveth a bird of good omen, and followeth the ship as it returned northward through fog and floating ice.

And a good south wind sprung up behind;
The Albatross did follow,
And every day, for food or play,
Came to the mariners' hollo!

In mist or cloud, on mast or shroud,
It perched for vespers nine;
Whiles all the night, through fog-smoke
        white,
Glimmered the white Moon-shine.'

56

The ancient Mariner inhospitably killeth the pious bird of good omen.

'God save thee, ancient Mariner!
From the fiends, that plague thee thus!—
Why look'st thou so?'—'With my cross-
        bow
I shot the ALBATROSS.

The Sun now rose upon the right:
Out of the sea came he,
Still hid in mist, and on the left
Went down into the sea.

And the good south wind still blew behind,
But no sweet bird did follow,
Nor any day for food or play
Came to the mariners' hollo!

His shipmates cry out against the ancient Mariner, for killing the bird of good luck.

And I had done a hellish thing,
And it would work 'em woe:
For all averred, I had killed the bird
That made the breeze to blow.
Ah wretch! said they, the bird to slay,
That made the breeze to blow!

But when the fog cleared off, they justify the same, and thus make themselves accomplices in the crime.

Nor dim nor red, like God's own head,
The glorious Sun uprist:
Then all averred, I had killed the bird
That brought the fog and mist.
'Twas right, said they, such birds to slay,
That bring the fog and mist.

The fair breeze continues; the ship enters the Pacific Ocean, and sails northward, even till it reaches the Line.

The fair breeze blew, the white foam flew,
The furrow followed free;
We were the first that ever burst
Into the silent sea.

The ship hath been suddenly becalmed.

Down dropt the breeze, the sails dropt
        down,
'Twas sad as sad could be;
And we did speak only to break
The silence of the sea![']

"... I shot the ALBATROSS." Illustration by Gustave Doré

Venturesome Seagoing Migrants

A powerful long-distance flier that rivals the albatross in its aerial abilities, the giant petrel, or fulmar, shown at left in flight off the Argentine coast, makes its home in Antarctica and ventures as far north as South America, South Africa and Australia. The largest of the petrels, it grows to a length of three feet, with a six- to eight-foot wingspan. The greater shearwater (below) is an even more venturesome migrant, regularly visiting the fishing fleets on the Grand Banks. Breeding only on the isolated South Atlantic islands of Gough and Tristan da Cunha, the birds travel as far north as Baffin Bay in the summer months, almost always flying just above the ocean's surface.

Herons and Their Kin

"He has taken a silent step, and with great care he advances; slowly does he raise his head from his shoulders, and now, what a sudden start! His formidable bill has transfixed a perch...." So Audubon described the painstakingly stealthy fishing technique of the great blue heron, one of the best known of the long-legged, long-necked birds of the order Ciconiiformes. Herons, along with egrets and their bashful relatives, bitterns, share a number of common characteristics—unwebbed feet, a comblike nail on the middle toe, serpentine necks and several patches of "powder" down feathers, which function as remarkable feather-cleaning equipment. Grooming usually takes place after a hard and dirty day of feeding. The birds rub their special feathers, releasing a fine white powder which they spread over their dirty areas. When all traces of the accumulated grime are covered, the birds wait a few moments and then, using the bill or the serrated nail of the big toe, comb their feathers out. A dash of oil from the preen gland completes the heron family toilet, restoring the birds' normally sleek appearance. It was the magnificence of their courtship plumage that led to the wide-scale slaughter of these birds, especially the egrets, some years ago. The passage of the rigid protection laws and a decline in the vogue for feathers in women's fashions have saved the birds from possible extinction.

Though their skinny legs and neck give herons a gaunt-looking appearance, they are actually hunting aids. Their methods of hunting food differ considerably. The blue heron is a stealthy stalker that uses its bill as pincers, as Audubon observed, and has an insatiable appetite for fish, even those that appear to be too large for its gullet. The gray and the white herons fish in the same way. The smaller, short-legged green heron, on the other hand, sometimes dives directly into the water after its prey. Black herons fish by spreading their wings over shallow water, creating a shadowy pool that attracts fish, and then waiting patiently for their prey to appear.

Storks often follow in the wake of plows during planting or threshers during a harvest, gobbling up snakes, lizards, frogs, grasshoppers, almost anything, including carrion, that is unearthed.

In Europe, storks have coexisted harmoniously with humans for centuries because of their legendary reputation as the bringers of babies and symbols of good luck (the German folkloric name for stork is *adebar*, meaning

"bearer of good fortune"). In the Near East the big birds are esteemed as "pilgrims of Mecca" because of their annual migrations over Islamic holy places. In their migratory flights, huge swarms of storks fly thousands of miles from Africa to nesting sites in Europe and the Near East.

The closely related ibises and spoonbills differ from most of the Ciconiiformes in that they have flattened or downward-curving bills and, like the storks, fly with necks extended rather than in the usual folded-back "S" configuration of herons. Medium- to large-sized waders, they, too, have distinctive feeding habits. Ibises search for fish by probing the water with their curving bills. Spoonbills swing their partly opened, clapperlike bills from side to side as they wade forward, snapping them shut whenever an insect, fish or crustacean touches their flattened bills.

The ibis and spoonbill family has extravagantly colored species. The black-and-white sacred ibis of Africa, the glossy ibis, which has an almost worldwide range, and white-faced glossy ibis of the New World are handsome birds, but the family beauty is unquestionably the spectacularly colored scarlet ibis, an inhabitant of the great northern swamplands of South America. Among spoonbills, the pink-and-white roseate is the most beautifully plumed. An American bird, one of six species, it was threatened with extinction some years ago when its feathers were widely used for fans, but as a protected species it is slowly making a comeback.

The flamingo, one of the most exquisitely colored of all birds, has a longer neck and legs in proportion to its body size than any other bird, and its color ranges from white to blushing pink. A flock of thousands of flamingos rising simultaneously from an African lake or a Caribbean lagoon is one of the most spectacular sights in nature. In the water at feeding time flamingos twist their necks around and hold their curved bills upside down. The bills have tooth-like edges that operate like strainers, filtering from the water millions of tiny plant and animal particles. In the course of a single day a flamingo may eat a tenth of its body weight in such minuscule portions. One element of a flamingo's diet, caratinoids, affects the pigmentation of the plumage. When they are abundant in the bird's food, the feathers maintain their rose color. When they are scarce, the big birds become paler; and when they are not present at all, the flamingo's fine feathers turn a drab off-white.

Greater flamingo

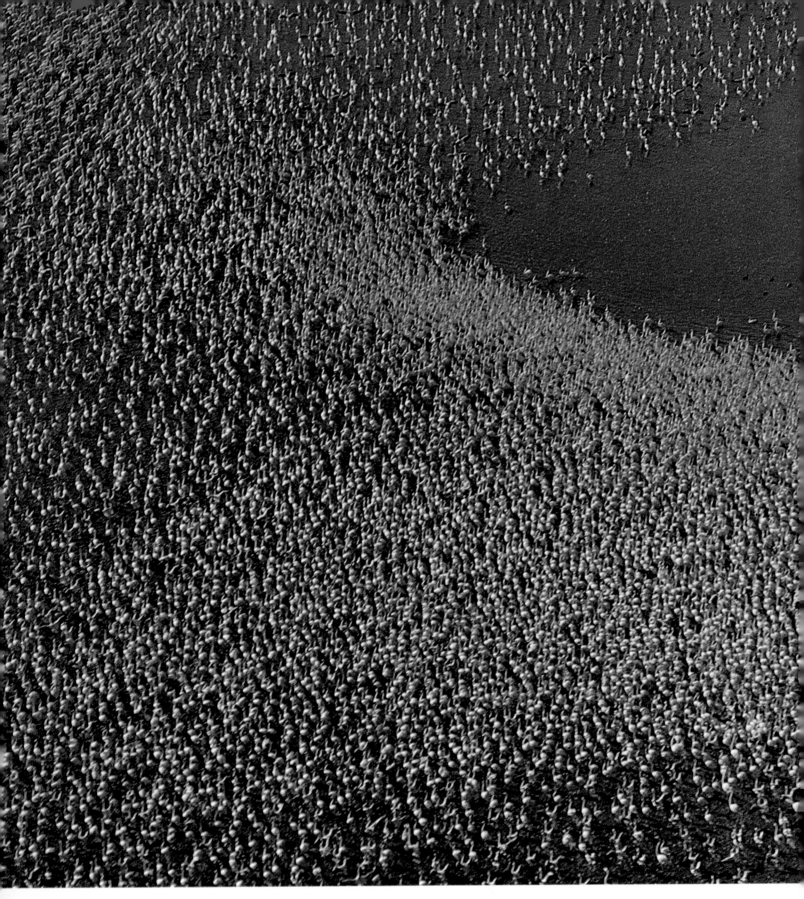

Brilliant Conclave of Big Pink Birds

Along the shores of Kenya's Lake Nakuru (left), thousands of flamingos present a dazzling avian pink tide. They are also found in southern Eurasia, Madagascar, the Caribbean and southern South America. The close-up below highlights both the flamingo's unusually long neck and its extraordinary bill. The extended neck is not the result of extra vertebrae but of the evolutionary lengthening of the individual bones. The bill, with its upper mandible fitting neatly into the lower one, is thrust upside down into the mud when the big bird feeds. In this position it traps much of the flamingo's diet of small frogs, shellfish, mollusks and aquatic plant life. Flamingos seem to thrive on such food. While not much is known about their life-spans in nature, they live as long as 30 years in captivity. Their individual longevity is impressive in the world of birds but pales in comparison to the species' geological age. Flamingo fossil remains date back more than 30 million years.

In an aerial ballet of delicate, pastel color and graceful motion, flamingos fly over the luxuriant landscape of their home in the Galápagos Islands. The Caribbean flamingos below exhibit an unusual nest-building technique. The nests, in the foreground, are made of heaped mud five to 18 inches high, molded into the shape of the base of a cone, with a shallow depression at the top for the single white egg. Both parents incubate the egg during its 28- to 32-day incubation period, then feed the hatchling with a special red-colored secretion, the high nutritional value of which compares with milk. The parents recognize their chick by its chirp and will refuse to feed any other young bird, no matter how much it might resemble theirs.

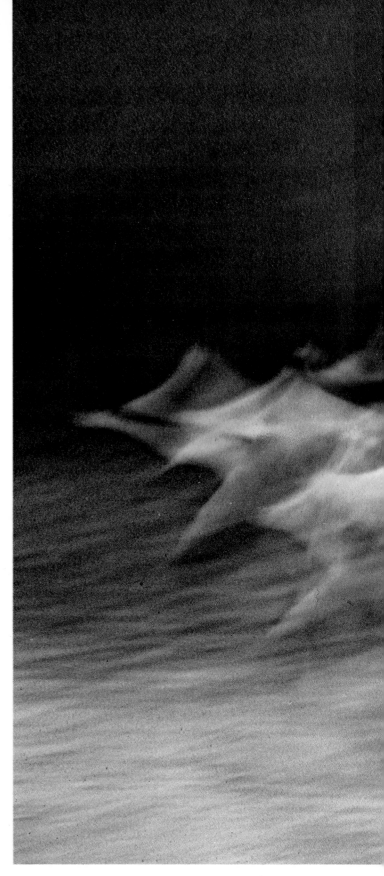

Flamingo Hunt *by Paul Zahl*

Paul Zahl, a noted biologist, prefers his hobby, photographing exotic animals and birds, to his work in the laboratory. In this excerpt from his book Flamingo Hunt, *Zahl describes·an expedition he and a companion took to the Bahamian island of Inagua at the behest of the National Audubon Society to band and photograph a large and very nervous flock of immature flamingos that had not yet learned to fly.*

The herd sensed that something was afoot and, with the distance differential reduced to perhaps 300 yards, began to show signs of serious concern. Individuals spread loosely around the periphery of the mass hastened hubward. Ranks tightened, and before long the flock had retreated as far as it could, hard against the densely mangroved lake's end. All heads were high out of the water by this time, and from each periscope glinted a pair of hard, fierce, frightened eyes—all fixed in the direction of the two human figures moving clumsily down the lake but closing in inexorably. The flock had three possible routes of escape: between me and the north shore; between John and the south shore; or up through the center between us. Our aim was to prevent the latter two but to encourage the first. And yet we couldn't leave the favored north passage too wide, for then the birds might flee back up the lake past the bay entrance, out of our clutches. The whole thing was tricky and suspenseful and required a slothful balance of forces. . . .

Soon we were within 100 yards of the knotted herd's front lines. The birds eddied this way and that; one felt the internal pressure would any second cause the boiler wall to give at its weakest point. But when I had reached a position just above the bay entrance John signaled me to stop. He continued, edging closer and easing the herd leftward, then gently goading them on uplake between me and the north shore. Beautifully according to plan they suddenly began oozing in the direction of what they thought was an escape hole. There was some crying and voicing, but not much; the birds seemed to direct their total energies into foot-and-swing action. A thousand pairs of sprinting legs made a sound suggestive of thunder-

less rainfall—one continuous wet murmur.

Why flightless flamingos are called "herds" by the natives was now clear: the movement was for all the world like that of a frightened herd of cattle. Even the dust was there—white spray from 2,000 legs slashing and splashing. From the air the flock would for a brief moment have resembled a lengthening teardrop. My presence just above the bay entrance left them no choice; into the bay they veered. By this time John was at my side, and we hurried in after so as to prevent any turnaround or retreat, although the word "hurry" to describe our movement across the lake swash is misleading. Our legs moved fast, to be sure, but mostly up and down; forward progress was anything but swift. The bay extended northward, but ever narrowing, a good quarter of a mile.

Now we had them, and as we closed in the herd dumbly

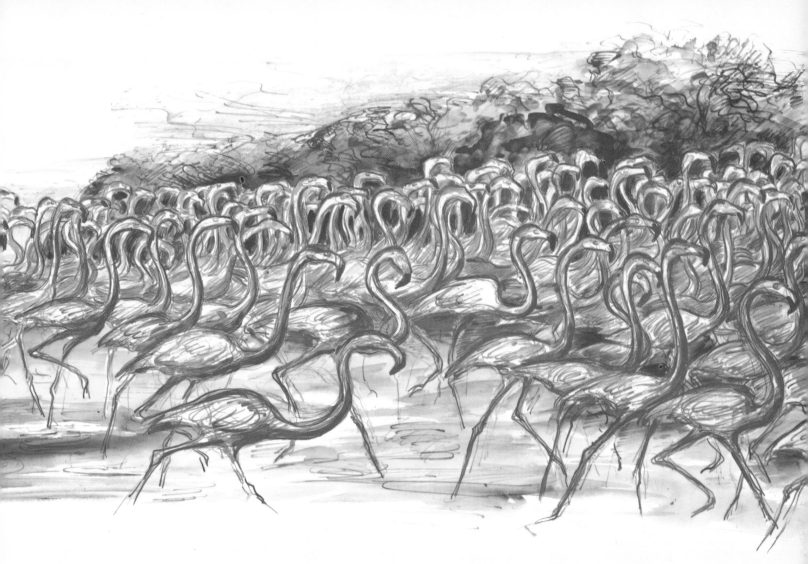

crowded into the bay's mangrove-walled V. It had been my vague impression that John's plan involved thus kraaling the herd tightly into that V and there somehow fencing them in with the cord. Then we could catch them singly for banding and release. But when John came over, handed me one end of the cord and began giving instructions I realized I was wrong. It was evident now that he was up to one of the oldest tricks in the flamingo hunter's book, long since described to me by Robbie Ferguson and others. The classic technique is for two or more men to corner a group of pre-flight waders, then, with each man holding the end of a fishline or facsimile, force the birds to stampede out across it. The birds rush blindly through the space between the two men, who then pull the cord taut and begin sweeping it powerfully forward. Under the right conditions two good huntsmen can break the legs of

dozens of flamingos within a few seconds and stun many more. These drop out of the stampede and float helplessly on the water. Once the rush for freedom has begun, there is no stopping it. The birds will keep hurling into the cord trap—some successfully hopping over, some successfully darting under, but many intercepting it squarely.

This plan is fine for native hunters in quest of fresh meat, but cruelly unsuited to a bird-banding mission. We'd have caught twenty or thirty birds, certainly, but half of them—legs or necks fractured—flapping great mortal flaps on the water . . . no, that was definitely not for us. Already I'd come to suspect that these adolescent birds were too wild and too nearly grown to be caught by any humane means. In bringing my 1,000 bands to Inagua I had envisioned a rookery with nestings small enough to make their capture easy and harmless. That period had long since passed. Also, at the time of the first break I had been within close-up view of the fleeing birds. I had looked well at those tall pink toothpicks; their fragility had struck at the heart of me.

Unaware of my thoughts, John was unrolling the cord and preparing for the advance on the herd, which cowered, restlessly trapped, a couple of hundred yards before us. I called him back and, opening my camera case, said we'd go closer to take some pictures, but to forget about the banding. As best I could I explained that to band ten or twenty birds would be of no value whatever; and, even if it were, the capture would involve mortal injury to a prohibitively large number of others. These birds were definitely too old. It would be like trying to brand a herd of nearly grown range cattle.

John gave me an uncomprehending look: here after strenuous herding we finally had got a thousand of the quarry nicely bottled up: we had these lovely shiny rings and a pair of pliers with which to apply them; certainly no man in his right mind would pass up this wonderful opportunity.

But I wasn't to be persuaded; we were going in closer with only a camera. Before long we were within a few hundred feet of the pink picket fence. There was no place the birds could go now without first pushing us out of their way, and this I hoped to avoid by a careful, limited approach. Some had already tried the mangrove, only to trip, fall and get their wings, legs and necks entangled in the arches. Closer and closer. Now I was within good range and had the camera to my eye. I hoped to take pictures fast, then retreat. But just as I snapped the shutter it happened. The dam broke.

They came at us like the front of a tidal wave—heads down, necks stretched out in front, wings beating wildly. Those horizontally held heads and necks resembled the down-spear charge of an ancient army, and it was this more than anything else that put the fear of God into me. To be trampled underfoot by birds seems like a silly thing, hardly possessing an element of danger. But these thousand wild creatures were nearly as tall as I and as dense as a solid wall.

John was about twenty feet to my left. I hastily glanced at him for a cue as to what to do. But just at that instant the tide hit us, obliterating John from sight. We were stones now on the shores of a raging pink sea. Suddenly my world was one of wings beating down and across my head and face, flamingo eyes and mouths inches from my own, necks spearing past. The first impact knocked me over, and I was knees-down on the ten-inch-deep bottom. Reflexively I turned my back on the stream and crouched with my head low. On and on they came, their webbed wet feet stamping up over my back, water from those alongside splashing up into my face. Out of the corner of my eye I could see only a speeding forest of pink bamboo.

The feeling swept over me that this could not be reality. It was so wholly removed from any other experience of my lifetime that for a moment I suspected my senses of deceit. Its duration was a year ten seconds long. Then it was over. I raised my head and saw the rear end of the herd tearing away in front of me. There was no lessening in speed until they were all across the bay and back into the primary lake.

Only then did I remember John and turn to where he had last stood. He was still there and most remarkably so.

He too had stooped and turned his back to the flood. But, instead of being mentally stunned as I had been, he had worked. As the birds swept by he had reached and plucked one after another by its neck or its legs or even its wings. Now he stood there with a grin on his face and with nine flamingos somehow stuck to him. He held the necks of three in each hand, had another couple tucked under his arms, was holding one between his legs. They were quiet, beaten, subdued by his grasp.

I had managed somehow to keep my camera above water during the charge, and the first thing I can remember doing was snapping John's picture. Then I walked over. Several of the birds whose necks he was gripping in his big strong hands seemed limp and dead. I repeated that there'd be no banding, and why not release his catch? He saw I was serious and dropped the load. Six of the nine immediately galloped off. Three slumped into the water, stunned or half choked. I picked their heads up and held them above the surface. They were still breathing and would recover.

John stood awkwardly by. His fine banding plan had been vetoed, and he was still wondering why. On an impulse I told him to untie his necklace and remove three bands. Then I reached into my wet pocket and handed him the pliers. I lifted the leg of one of the flamingos and held it above the water. John's gloom evaporated. He quickly pliered open one of the aluminum rings. Then with the uncertain sureness of a bridegroom he placed the metal on the finger-thick flamingo leg and bent it back into circular shape. We did this to all three birds, which soon revived, stood up and loped away in the direction of the main flock. With each lope we could see the sparkle of something shiny. . . .

Three banded birds can have no scientific significance. But, should you ever run across a flamingo wearing a serial-numbered ankle bracelet, I'd certainly like to know.

Scarlet Ibises

The beautiful scarlet ibis ranges through tropical South America from Brazil to northwestern Venezuela, although it sometimes roams as far north as the West Indies. Traveling in large flocks (right), ibises fly with their necks and featherless faces thrust straight forward and their long, slender legs stretched out behind them. The beautiful plumage of these birds has invited the depredations of man, for over the years they have been slaughtered without mercy by men greedy for their brilliant feathers. Scarlet ibises have also been killed by primitive Indians for meat, which some tribes apparently relish, though most people would find it too odorous and oily. Scarlet ibises nest as well as roost in coastal mangrove swamps (overleaf), turning the foliage into a dazzling display of color.

A Plumed God and a Legend

Since the early Middle Ages the European white stork (right) has been regarded as a bird of good omen. Its legendary reputation as the deliverer of babies is among the more persistent myths of cultural history. In earlier times, in some rural villages from Holland eastward to the Balkans, almost every house boasted its own stork. The birds are still encouraged to nest by homeowners, and as a result the species has flourished as it has nowhere else in its breeding range, which extends across Asia into the Far East. In France, for example, where stork mythology is not a part of local folklore, the white stork has ceased to thrive where it was once plentiful. The sacred ibis (opposite), a cousin of the storks, is another ancient bird whose fossil records, like the storks', go back some 50 million years. The sacred ibis, an African species, was venerated by the ancient Egyptians and became an integral part of their religion and hieroglyphics. The painted stork (below) is an Asian species that, like all storks, subsists primarily on a diet of insects and fish, though it eats small birds and rodents as well.

Versatile Herons

The herons constitute one of the most widespread families of wading birds, with 64 species that range through Eurasia, the Americas, Africa, Australia, Madagascar, New Zealand and some oceanic islands. Three of the 13 American species are pictured here: the snowy egret (left), whose delicate, ethereal aspect qualifies it as the most beautiful of the herons; the great blue heron (below), one of the larger family members and a versatile creature equally at home on small streams, upland meadows, lakeshores, salt- and freshwater marshes, shallow bays and even crop fields; and the green heron (opposite, below), one of the smallest members of the heron family. Unlike many other herons, which catch their prey by standing still, little egrets (opposite, above) stalk their prey in shallow ponds or mud flats. Approaching cautiously, they seize fish with a lightning jab of the bill or scare up prey by vibrating a foot.

The snowy egret (above) is a less patient fisher than other herons and accelerates the hunting process by stirring up the pond bottom with its feet, then rushing about seizing the small fish, crabs or insects it has flushed. The great blue heron (right), often called the blue crane, is easily distinguished from true cranes when in flight. The great blue flies with a folded neck, while all cranes keep their necks outstretched when they are airborne.

76

Without their nuptial head plumage, which molts after the breeding season, little egrets (above) look pretty much like any other members of the heron family. The green heron (right) also undergoes a radical change when it begins courtship. The irises of its eyes turn from yellow to orange, and its yellow legs become coral pink.

Spoonbills

The Eurasian spoonbill (opposite and above) can be found over a wide area across Europe and India. The spoonbill flies with its neck straight and wings flapping steadily (above). Spoonbills wade through the shallow waters of marshes with their half-open bills partly submerged, swinging their heads from side to side and closing their bills on anything edible that comes their way. Their diet consists primarily of small crustaceans, insects, fish, amphibians and worms, along with some vegetable matter. A close-up of the roseate spoonbill (left) shows its peculiarly shaped but very serviceable bill. Multitudes of roseate spoonbills once nested from the Gulf Coast of the United States southward to Argentina and Chile, but now they have almost been exterminated by man. Urbanization along the Florida coast is destroying the feeding grounds of the few remaining roseates. They are adaptable birds, however, and sometimes seek out new environments, nesting in mixed colonies with wood storks and egrets.

The Eurasian spoonbill (above) has the characteristic white plumage of its other Old World relatives. Like all spoonbills, it is a sociable bird and likes to nest in homogeneous spoonbill colonies. The female usually lays three dull-white, brown-spotted eggs, which are incubated by both parents for about 24 days until they hatch. The parents feed the young by regurgitating food they have caught. As they grow, the hatchlings learn to push their bills down their parents' throats, literally taking the food right out of their mouths.

Silhouetted against an Indian
sunset, a quintet of Eurasian
spoonbills presents a haunting
picture. When they flock together,
spoonbills communicate by means
of grunting, croaking or clacking
their bills. In Asia, spoonbills often
nest high in trees; in Europe, they are
more likely to choose reeds and
other marsh plants close to the
ground or over the water.

80

Ospreys

Circling 50 to 100 feet in the sky, an osprey spots a fish below, hovers an instant and then plummets down with its wings half closed, feet extended and talons wickedly splayed. Seconds later it splashes feet first into the water, sending up a plume of spray, and disappears beneath the water. In a few moments it breaks surface again, with a glistening fish clutched beneath its brown-and-white body like a torpedo. The only raptor, or bird of prey, that is exclusively a fisherman, the osprey is a soaring, powerful flier of relatively large size—from 20 to 24 inches in length and a five- to six-foot wingspan—armed with lethal talons and opposable outer toes that can be instantly reversed, making it possible to seize and hold with two toes in front and two behind. In addition, the birds have special pads beneath their talons, coated with short, stiff spines to improve their already deadly grip. Ospreys feed only on fish, preferably trout, that they catch themselves. Ospreys will sometimes eat fish they have not caught themselves but only if the prey is unspoiled. One of the few dangers ospreys face is the possibility of drowning when they sink their claws in a fish so large that it might pull them under before they can disengage their talons.

Inhabiting seacoasts and the shores of large lakes and rivers throughout the world (with the exception of New Zealand and Antarctica), ospreys are impressive nest builders, diligently fashioning bulky five- and six-foot structures out of sticks and branches, most often in dead trees or on cliffs, occasionally on the ground and, often enough to outrage power companies, on telephone and power poles. Ornithologist Roger Tory Peterson tells of an osprey that carried off a garbage-can cover, planted it high on a power-line pole and nested in it. All was fine, with supporting branches apparently insulating the metal top, until rain filled the cover, causing it to tip over and black out the neighborhood for an hour. In less precarious surroundings, osprey nests are used over and over, often by the same pair, with the record for observed continual usage being 40 years. Each pair usually produces three eggs, which are white speckled with red and brown. Incubation takes about five weeks and is followed by another two months of close parental supervision before the young birds reach the fledgling stage, returning to the nest only at night until they are mature enough to fly off on their own.

Besides the ospreys there are many other raptors that are sea and freshwater fish eaters. The eagles are members of the genus *Haliaeëtus*, which includes many birds that feed predominantly on fish. Some sea eagles prefer to feast on carrion—or to pirate from other birds—while a few species, like the African fish eagle, are omnivorous predators. Largest of the group, with a wingspan of between seven and eight feet, is Steller's sea eagle. Found mostly in northern Japan and parts of Siberia, this great raptor feeds on other birds as well as fish and mammals as large as the Arctic fox. The genus's best-known member, the bald eagle, is generally a fish-eater. Like the osprey, it is regularly found along seacoasts and inland lakes and streams.

Kingfishers and dippers, although not related to the birds of prey, are also stream-dwellers. Kingfishers are small (four to 18 inches), iridescent birds whose 80 or so species are found throughout the temperate and tropical regions of the world. Many are not actually fish-catchers and do not live near water. These species, however, maintain the family penchant for sitting patiently, then swooping down on their prey. Those kingfishers that do fish use the same strategy, perching on a branch over a stream or hovering 20 or 30 feet overhead, wings beating rapidly, before pitching down for a quick strike.

The proprietors of fish hatcheries in Europe regard the kingfishers as useful aids to the environment, because they take only the smallest, weakest fish and keep the schools from becoming overpopulated. In the Orient, though, the birds are unwelcome at fish farms, and breeders sometimes go to the extreme of covering their ponds with netting to keep the kingfishers from poaching. All members of the kingfisher family nest in holes—in the banks of streams, termite mounds or rotted tree trunks. Before mating, both the male and female birds dig their underground breeding nest, which may lie as much as 10 feet from the entrance. As a prelude to courtship, the male kingfisher often brings his mate a "wedding present"—appropriately, a fish.

Most unusual of all, perhaps, among water-feeding birds is a relatively small family of four species of wrenlike songbirds known as dippers, water ouzels or "water walkers." Feeding mostly on insects and their larvae, these remarkable creatures do not trot across the surface, as the jacanas do, but actually forage the bottoms of fast-moving inland streams. Powered by short, stubby wings, swimming and even planing down against the current, dippers can reach depths of 10 to 20 feet below the surface and stay submerged for half a minute or so.

Young ospreys

Two Regal Marine Predators

The osprey, or fish hawk (left), and the African fish eagle (opposite and picture sequence below) are two consummate fishers among the Falconiformes, an order of birds of prey. The osprey, which closely resembles the large hawks and eagles, is one of the most widely distributed of all birds, living along the coasts and near the larger lakes and rivers of the continental land masses of the world, except Antarctica and New Zealand, as well as on many remote islands. The African fish eagle ranges throughout most of southern Africa and is a familiar sight around Lake Victoria and other inland waters, where it occasionally contends with an osprey for a fresh catch. Both birds subsist primarily on fish caught in swooping, feet-first dives into the water. The fish eagle, unlike the osprey, will sometimes travel miles from its normal habitat to feast on carrion. Fish eagles also kill young water birds for food.

Ospreys build massive nests of sticks and twigs (above) and often use the same ones repeatedly, sometimes for as long as 40 years running. Tops of very high, dead trees or telephone poles are preferred as nesting sites, though nesting on the poles can disrupt service and has prompted some utility firms to erect special poles with wagon wheels laid flat on top to attract the birds. The osprey population has declined drastically along America's eastern coast as a result of eating pesticide-contaminated fish.

84

In the three-picture sequence at left, an African fish eagle descends to water level, on the lookout for dinner (far left). Eying a fish, the fish eagle drops into the water with a splash to snatch it (center), drags it along the surface for several yards before hoisting the catch aloft (left) and returns home (above) with a treat for its eaglets.

Kingfishers and Dippers

The malachite kingfisher (above) is a solitary creature, rarely seen with others of its kind except during courtship. Though the malachite is one of the smaller species, most kingfishers are husky birds with large heads, short legs and a strong bill resembling a spear tip. Most species are true water birds that dive for fish, but some hunt insects and small animals far from water. One genus name, *Alcyon*, derives from a figure in Greek mythology, Alcyone, who drowned herself after her husband died in a shipwreck. Out of pity, the gods changed both into kingfishers, and it was believed that the birds hatched their eggs on a nest floating in the sea during the calm of the winter solstice—

14 days of tranquil seas proclaimed by Zeus for the kingfishers' nesting. The legend led to the association of the term "halcyon" with peaceful times.

Another loner, the Eurasian dipper (opposite), so named for its habit of vigorously bobbing its head 40 to 60 times a minute while on land, is the only purely aquatic perching bird in North America. It is capable of "flying" underwater, propelled by its stubby, rounded wings. Dippers also walk the bottoms of stream beds in search of insects and small fish for food. Special flaps close over each nostril to prevent water inhalation when submerged, and an enlarged gland provides oil for waterproofing.

86

A Eurasian dipper (above) flies past one of its characteristic nesting sites—behind the downrushing torrent of a waterfall. The slate-gray Eurasian dipper, which subsists mainly on a diet of water insects and their larvae as well as on sand hoppers, inhabits mountainous areas of Europe, North Africa and Asia.

Waders

Through the rich belt of marine life that lies between the tidelines they scamper, tails twitching, long legs moving nimbly, thin, sharp bills alert and ready to strike. The smallest of the waders is sparrow-sized; the largest is as big as a chicken. Most have brown backs fading to a lighter color underneath, making it difficult to distinguish the different species. These are the waders—oystercatchers and tattlers, curlews and godwits, turnstones, sandpipers, jacanas, surfbirds, phalaropes and even inland birds, snipes and woodcocks. All are members of a widespread order of inland, shore and offshore birds, the Charadriiformes, and all have developed remarkably individual techniques and implements for harvesting the riches of the tidal zones and marshlands.

Oystercatchers have long, blunt, vertically flattened orange bills that they wield with great skill. They are capable not only of slicing through the clamping muscle of partially opened oysters, clams and mussels but also of prying limpets off rocks, crushing crabs and probing mud shoals for sand fleas, worms and shrimps.

Long-billed curlews use their eight-inch bills like forceps to extract shellfish from tidal flats and beaches. Turnstones, as their name suggests, are able to turn stones, sticks and other beach debris in search of food. Short-necked, chunky birds, they have short, slightly upturned bills, natural crowbars that permit them to flip over shells and half-dried patches of seaweed in their endless search for marine life underneath.

Woodcocks and other snipes are migrant waders that have moved inland, where their delicately mottled coloring provides excellent camouflage. Their eyes, set on the sides of their heads, have evolved to furnish almost 360-degree vision. The basic diet of these avid eaters is worms, and a single woodcock may devour half its weight in worms in a day. Snipes, which favor marshy areas, feed on snails, small crustaceans and insect larvae. An elusive, nocturnal bird, the woodcock is much esteemed as a table delicacy. The most spectacular of the marsh birds in terms of locomotion is the jacana, or lily-trotter. The jacana's quarter-of-a-pound weight is distributed evenly over the broad base created by its elongated toes and toenails, allowing it to scamper across a floating field of lily pads or water hyacinths with surefooted ease.

At the other end of the evolutionary scale are two seafarers, surfbirds and phalaropes. Stocky, grayish in color, surfbirds are remarkably long-range migrators that inhabit kelp-covered rocks and breakwater reefs. They are distributed along the Pacific littoral from Alaska to the Straits of Magellan, where they feed on mollusks and crustaceans. In Alaska, where they breed, their diet changes to insects. Phalaropes are seagoing birds with ducklike, waterproof belly feathers and partially webbed feet. In winter they may be found miles out in the Pacific, devouring the tiny marine creatures in buoyant masses of seaweed.

Plovers form another large group of waders that have a worldwide distribution and short, somewhat plump bodies and pigeonlike bills, which are considerably shorter than those of other waders. These sturdy birds inhabit beaches, mud flats and grassy fields. In flocks of hundreds, they often track the fringes of receding waves, plucking small sea creatures from the damp sand. Most intriguing of all plovers is the wrybill of New Zealand, which is the only bird in the world with a laterally bent beak—always to the right—an evolutionary twist of fate for which scientists have no satisfactory explanation.

All plovers are accomplished actors, feigning injury and fluttering helplessly in order to lure intruders away from their nesting areas. On the nest, plovers and lapwings demonstrate many characteristics common to waders. Most nest on the ground in simple depressions or hollows and lay four eggs that are pyriform, or pear-shaped, so that they fit together like the sections of an orange and can be incubated by a single bird. Hatchlings appear after about three weeks' incubation covered with a speckled, camouflage down. They are active from birth and leave the nest within hours, running behind their parents in search of their own food. They are usually fledged in a month's time.

Avocets and stilts are the most elegant waders of all, having not only very long legs but also elongated necks and slender, gracefully sculpted bodies. Wading through the shallows, avocets feed by sweeping their partially open bills from side to side through the water. Stilts, with their exceedingly long legs—longer in proportion to body size than those of any other bird except the flamingo—use their straight bills to probe the mud for shrimps, crustaceans, insects and other marine edibles. Both stilts and avocets are found in warm climates, both breed colonially, usually in marshlands or at the edges of lagoons, and both are often forced to shore up their nests to protect their eggs from rising waters. On the nest itself the stilt solves the problem of its long legs by folding them back against themselves to the rear.

Black-winged stilt

Sandpipers and Avocets

When the tide goes out at Assoteague, an island off the coast of Maryland and Virginia, it is dinnertime for swarms of sandpipers (below). Scurrying across the wet sand, they busily probe for small crustaceans, mollusks and marine insects that make up their diet. Sandpipers are sociable birds, willingly sharing their beaches with other small shorebirds and often allowing humans to approach within five or six feet of them before taking off. They are found in most parts of the world and make prodigious annual migrations, some species traveling up to 6,000 miles.

Their noisy, cocky-looking cousin, the American avocet (opposite), is anything but friendly during the breeding season. When any avian intruder goes near their nesting areas in wetlands or alkaline lakes of the western United States and Canada, the big birds rush out angrily, charging threateningly at the invader. When there are no eggs or young to defend, though, avocets are quite tame and indifferent to intruders—an attitude that has made them easy game for hunters and, together with the destruction of their habitats, has made them rare in eastern North America.

The American avocet (right) disappeared completely from its former habitat in the wetlands of the southeastern United States but has mysteriously reappeared in recent years. Its unique turned-up bill serves as a filter to sort out the tiny shellfish and insects that are the avocet's principal food.

Special Equipment

The waders on these pages are distinguished by some highly specialized physical equipment, used for some highly specialized jobs. The skimmer is the only bird in the world with a protruding lower bill. Slicing the surface of the water, a black skimmer (above) dips its lower bill into the water in search of food. The moment the submerged mandible strikes a passing shrimp or small fish, the razor-sharp upper bill clamps shut. The bills are also used in clacking prenuptial rites, demonstrated by a black skimmer pair at left before an attentive audience of downy chicks. The stiletto-sharp bill of the oystercatcher (opposite, right) is also a formidable tool that can deftly open oysters or other bivalves. The adaptations of the jacana (opposite, left) are its extra-long feet and toenails that enable the bird to walk daintily across lily pads or other floating vegetation in pursuit of insects and minnows.

Without its oversized, ungainly-looking feet the African jacana stalking insects in Lake Nakuru, Kenya (above), would be unable to get around so nimbly on the lily pads or water hyacinths that cover its habitat. Jacanas range throughout the tropical and subtropical regions of the world and are also known as lotus birds and lily-trotters.

Oystercatchers (right) are large, boisterous birds with sharp beaks, shaped like oyster-shucking knives, that are capable of prying limpets from rocks and crushing small crabs, as well as opening the shells of bivalves. They range along the seacoasts and the shores of large rivers of all the continents except Antarctica. When tides are high and their food supply is submerged, oystercatchers rest, standing in solemn rows with their heads to the wind.

Gulls and Terns

Gulls are versatile and tireless contributors to their environment. As scavengers they are efficient garbage collectors. Noisy, quarrelsome and aggressive, they steal the prey and cannibalize the eggs and hatchlings of other birds, and occasionally, when no other food is available, they even eat the young of other gulls. But, as exterminators of pests, they have sometimes rendered great services to man. In 1848, for instance, California gulls destroyed swarms of invading crickets that threatened crops in Utah, and again in 1947 in Scotland, black-headed gulls turned back a plague of caterpillars. In some places gulls are so highly esteemed for cleaning debris from beaches and coastal waters that they are protected from the predations of man by law.

Although they are the best known of all water birds and are usually associated with shores and seaports, some gulls range far inland. They are found in almost every quarter of the earth, including the polar regions, wherever land and sea meet. And although they have webbed feet and oil glands to waterproof their feathers, most gulls are not true oceangoing birds and are never very far from land. Their appetites are enormous and not at all specialized. When they hunt, gulls frequently alight on the water, feeding as they float. And they exercise remarkable ingenuity in getting at difficult food. When a gull finds a mussel or clam in shallow water, it may fly high over a rocky area with its prize and drop the shell repeatedly until it cracks. So effective, in fact, are gulls at getting what they want—and thus surviving—that in some areas they have become a serious problem, menacing other birds, striking airplanes and fouling buildings.

Long-winged, with streamlined bodies and generally square tails, the world's more than 40 species of gulls are, along with nearly as many species of terns, members of the Laridae family in the order Charadriiformes. Ranging in size from the greater black-backed gull, a handsome bird some two and a half feet long with a wingspan approaching six feet, to the little gull, 10 inches long, with a 21-inch wingspan, they are highly gregarious, gathering in noisy colonies of hundreds of thousands of members. Gulls are not very particular about their nesting sites or building materials, using whatever is at hand—grass, feathers, twigs, fish line and other debris. Both sexes help in incubating the two or three eggs, which hatch in about three to four weeks. If the eggs are lost, the female gull will quickly lay again—another survival mechanism—replacing her lost broods, if necessary, as often as three or four times. Newly hatched chicks remain in the nest until nearly full-grown, protected by camouflage suits of speckled brown down. Because predators and gulls feed on the young of other gulls, however, only one of four or five hatchlings may live to fly at the age of eight weeks.

Though closely related to gulls, terns are generally smaller, more graceful birds, with brightly colored, delicately sculpted bills. Some terns have forked tails, which accounts for their nickname of sea swallow. Though a few species are freshwater birds, most terns are shoreline hunters, swooping, hovering, occasionally plunging but only rarely landing on the water. In general they are not as avid hunters as gulls are, though they do steal from other birds and they are habitually quarrelsome. With their own kind, terns are gregarious nesters, swarming together in colonies of millions of birds, with two and even three pairs sharing a single square yard of prime nesting turf. One species, the Arctic tern, flies as a loner. Cruising solo from the land of the midnight sun to the Antarctic summer, the small bird spends more of its lifetime in daylight hours than any other living creature—roughly 10 months of the year.

Even more aggressive are the birds of a small family closely related to the gulls and terns—the skuas and jaegers. They are perhaps the most courageous of all birds when defending their nests. Skuas are found in both hemispheres, especially near the poles in the Arctic and Antarctic, where they breed. Keenly predatory, skuas and jaegers are the hawks, falcons and even the vultures of the sea, often robbing other nests and omnivorously eating garbage, other birds, berries, eggs (especially those of penguins), lemmings and other small mammals, insects, carrion and, if they straggle off, chicks of their own kind.

The most fascinating of all birds allied with gulls and terns are the skimmers, or scissorbills. They are rather small birds, growing to a length of about 20 inches. They have two unusual features—vertically slit pupils in their eyes, like cats, and protruding lower jaws that are not only considerably longer than the upper bills but are flexible as well. Rarely touching the water with their bodies, the skimmers fish along calm, coastal rivers and streams, lower beak razoring just beneath the surface to scoop up any small fish or crustaceans. The birds skim at dawn and dusk and during the night, racing upstream for a quick run and then turning and skimming downstream, pausing on the riverbank periodically to rest and eat their catch.

Ring-billed gulls

Shore Patrol

Herring gulls, those noisy gray-and-white shore patrols of Europe and North America, are the most widespread and best-known members of their family. They cover the water-fronts of large seaports and small fishing villages from New York to Helsinki and also range far inland, along lakes and rivers. They always travel in screaming swarms, clouds of them trailing in the wake of fishing boats or garbage scows or in migratory groups of tens of thousands that darken the skies. Scavengers of a high order, they render a great service in cleaning beaches, harbors and lake and river shores. Wherever they gather, whether policing a garbage dump in Martha's Vineyard (above) or waiting for dinner on the roof of a Nantucket fisherman's shack (opposite, below), herring gulls are invariably in groups.

Like its cousins the gregarious gulls, the Arctic tern (right) gathers in flocks to breed. But the terns are quarrelsome with their own kind, although they willingly share their nesting sites with other species of birds. Arctic terns are marvelous fliers, and their incredible annual journeys take them as far afield as Point Barrow, close to the North Pole, to Ross Sea, deep in Antarctica—easily the longest migration of any living creature.

Ducks

The most familiar, varied and widespread of all ducks, mallards belong to a large group of surface feeders in the family Anatidae, which includes geese and swans. Tipped forward, in a marsh or pool, yellow webbed feet pedaling hard, mallards and their kin devour vast quantities of tiny surface and subsurface aquatic plants, the roots, stems and seeds of larger ones; nuts, fruits, insects, including mosquitoes and their larvae and pupae; certain invertebrates such as earthworms and crayfish; and, of course, bread crusts and crumbs.

Despite their voracious hunger, from man's point of view, mallards have been a major resource. Over the centuries, both in their wild state and as the progenitors of most strains of modern domestic ducks, including the familiar barnyard quacker, the Peking duck, they have provided countless tons of flesh, eggs and feathers for human consumption and use.

In migratory, mating and molting habits, the surface feeders—including such species as the black duck, the exquisitely hued wood duck, pintails and teals—show a remarkable capacity for adaptation, especially in proximity with man. The annual migration begins relatively late in the fall in their Canadian habitats, where great flocks of mallards and blacks rise almost vertically from the water in characteristically high-angled takeoffs and head south and east, sometimes at speeds of 40 to 60 miles per hour down through the Mississippi Valley and out along the Gulf Coast. It is there, in early spring or even later, on the way home, that pairing occurs, with an intricate courtship ballet, launched by the richly colored male.

After they reach the nesting area the speckled female builds the nest. The birds then separate and the female incubates the eggs and raises the ducklings alone. This is not a case of deliberate neglect by the drake, for it is at nesting time that the ducks lose their flight feathers, at once becoming grounded and easy game for predators. During this vulnerable time, in their efforts to insure safety, the ducks may sometimes resort to underwater diving, as their young ducklings will do whenever danger threatens. About a month later the male and female regain their flight feathers and the ability to fly, but the drake's handsome nuptial plumage does not reappear until much later, in the autumn or early winter.

Not all surface feeders follow the broad behavioral patterns of the group. Shovelers, or shovel ducks, have over-sized bills, which they use to scoop up ooze and pond water in order to strain for edibles with comblike teeth, much as flamingos do. And the torrent ducks of the high Andes, which are also classified as surface feeders, paddle like white-water racers down rushing streams, gobbling insect larvae and mollusks, and then fly back upstream for another run.

The diving ducks (redheads, canvasbacks, ringnecks and scaup) and the sea ducks (goldeneyes, eiders and scoters) form another great Anatidae family grouping. With shorter, broader bills than the surface feeders, legs set a bit farther back and a more leisurely, surface-churning style of takeoff, these birds are underwater feeders. A few of them are able to dive to depths of 40 feet. The redheads and canvasbacks are generally found in fresh or brackish waters, while the goldeneyes and eiders prefer saltier regions. Canvasbacks, wintering on the wild celery beds around Chesapeake Bay, are favorites of sportsmen and gourmets alike. The eiders range far north, encircling the North Pole and skirting the land masses of Siberia, Alaska, Iceland, Greenland and the Scandinavian countries. During the summer months eiders migrate to inland areas as well, to freshwater ponds and lakes. The eiders are famous, of course, for their extraordinarily soft, lightweight down, which they use to line their nests and man has used for years to stuff pillows, quilts and cold-weather gear. Harvested in Iceland, Canada and other northern countries, eider feathers are so light that it takes 35 to 40 nests to produce a single pound of commercial down.

For the most part, eiders feed on mollusks and crabs and have short, heavy bills to help catch and pin their prey and powerful stomach muscles that are capable of pulverizing a crab's shell. The most skilled of the divers in terms of design are the mergansers, which are predominantly fish eaters. Slenderer and more streamlined than other diving ducks, they have long, narrow, cylindrical bills needled with toothlike serrations. These pseudo teeth, which are swept backward along the bill, are designed to catch—and hold—one fish at a time. With their ability to dive and to submerge without leaving a ripple, the mergansers are among the ablest of avian fishers.

The black-headed duck of southern South America has the sneaky habit of laying its oversized eggs in the nests of other birds and leaving the incubation and upbringing to the hapless foster parents.

Mandarin drake

Surf Scoters and Old Squaws

Ducks are among the most gregarious of birds, congregating in flocks of as many as 10,000 and more. Below, a huge convoy of surf scoters surrounds one lonely scaup floating in the center of the group. The surf scoter likes to feed over mussel beds close to the shore and ventures inland only to breed or to escape a storm. Scaup also gather in the waters above mussel beds. Because of their fishy diets, surf scoters and scaup have coarse, gamy flesh and are disdained by duck hunters. Vegetable-eating canvasback ducks (close relatives of the scaup), on the other hand, have long been esteemed as table delicacies. In common with all marine ducks, both surf scoters and scaup are good divers. A species called the old squaw, for example, has been caught in fishermen's nets as far down as 100 feet.

An aerial display of thousands of mallard and pintail ducks (above) darkens the sky over the Camas National Wildlife Refuge in eastern Idaho, long a favorite nesting area for many species of waterfowl. Among ducks the South African cape widgeon (right) is an unusually social bird. It often travels in vast flocks numbering more than 10,000. When they are not feeding or flying, cape widgeons stand together in ranks, resting or sleeping. Three of the four ducks pictured are standing on one leg, which is apparently a most comfortable pose for ducks.

101

The Downy Eiders

Of all the various species of sea ducks, the eider is the best known and the most widespread, with a circumpolar range in the northern hemisphere. It may also be the most numerous, traveling in huge flocks. The eider prefers to nest in colonies, and, in common with nearly all other ducks, the female lines its nest with down plucked from her own breast. In the eider's case, the down is so extraordinarily soft that it has become a valuable commercial commodity and is literally harvested by man. The male spectacled eider, which ranges through Arctic Siberia and Alaska, is shown above, while at the right a young eider surveys the scene on Amchitka Island, Alaska. It will take a duckling about seven weeks before learning to fly.

King and commoner in the eider society are represented here. Above is the male king eider. And at left, still within their large, greenish eggs, are a couple of embryo common eiders. When the ducklings emerge, their main protection against predators will be their camouflaging coloration, the warnings of their mother and, after they make the trek to the water, their diving ability. Diving is more than an escape tactic. Eiders must dive for the fish and mollusks that are their principal food.

103

Sitting Ducks

The white-faced tree ducks (above), members of the perching duck family, are distantly related to the Egyptian goose, which stands in their midst. Tree ducks are found in tropical regions. They are able to perch easily on branches, and their natural resting position is an upright stance, in contrast to that of other waterfowl, which usually squat. Perching ducks spend more time in trees than do any other ducks. They are equipped with long, sharp, strong claws, and they have a well developed hind toe. The wood duck (opposite), whose perfect reflection in the still water creates an exotic design, has a wide range, extending from

Florida to southern Canada. These ducks are such favorites with the breeders of domestic waterfowl that they are tolerated as free-flying, free-loading visitors. Wood ducks prefer to make their nests in tree hollows near small freshwater ponds, lakes and inland streams. They are close relatives of the Mandarin duck of eastern Asia and Japan. But, despite the close relationship, the Mandarin duck will never breed in captivity with the wood duck nor with any other species. The reason for the Mandarin's unusually selective mating preference is believed to be a peculiar malformation of one of its chromosomes.

The Mallard Clan

The mallard (above) is the ancestor of most domestic ducks including the familiar Peking ducks on the opposite page. During courtship it goes through a number of unusual displays. In one, the drake churns up a small shower of water in front of him with a sudden movement of his bill. As a preliminary to mating, both birds move their heads up and down, as though they were preparing to take flight. During the act of mating, which takes place (as with all waterfowl) on the water, the female duck is completely submerged. While the ducks are sitting on the eggs, the drakes, who take no interest in raising the young, often gather on a nearby lake. They will pursue any female duck that flies from the nest to feed or preen herself. At left, three mallard ducklings share a patch of ground with their cousin, a domestic duckling.

Contrary to their name, the domestic Peking ducks (below) are not wholly Asian. They are descended, as are almost all other commercially bred ducks, from the ancestral mallard, a worldwide species. They all bear the curling feathers on the upper tail that are the mark of their heritage. To make matters more confusing, the only Old World domestic ducks that were not bred from mallards are those developed by the Chinese. On Long Island, New York, literally millions of white Pekings are commercially bred on vast duck farms and sold under the name of Long Island ducklings.

King Solomon's Ring *by Konrad Lorenz*

It was said that King Solomon could converse with animals, and certainly men of lesser wisdom have managed to establish some sort of communication with household pets and even wild creatures. Dr. Konrad Lorenz, the distinguished zoologist and Nobel Prize winner, believes that the higher orders of animals have distinct means of communication that a human observer can learn and use. In his studies the Austrian-born scientist has succeeded in becoming an animal's friend, leader and surrogate mother. In this excerpt from King Solomon's Ring *Lorenz tells how, at the expense of his dignity, he convinced a brood of mallard ducklings that he was really their mother. The photographs show that his approach works equally well with young geese.*

I was experimenting at one time with young mallards to find out why artificially incubated and freshly hatched ducklings of this species, in contrast to similarly treated

greylag goslings, are unapproachable and shy. Greylag goslings unquestioningly accept the first living being whom they meet as their mother, and run confidently after him. Mallards, on the contrary, always refused to do this. If I took from the incubator freshly hatched mallards, they invariably ran away from me and pressed themselves in the nearest dark corner. Why? I remembered that I had once let a muscovy duck hatch a clutch of mallard eggs and that the tiny mallards had also failed to accept this foster-mother. As soon as they were dry, they had simply run away from her and I had trouble enough to catch these crying, erring children. On the other hand, I once let a fat white farmyard duck hatch out mallards and the little wild things ran just as happily after her as if she had been their real mother. The secret must have lain in her call-note, for, in external appearance, the domestic duck was quite as different from a mallard as was the muscovy; but what she had in common with the mallard (which, of course, is the wild progenitor of our farmyard duck) were her vocal expressions. Though, in the process of domestication, the duck has altered considerably in colour pattern and body form, its voice has remained practically the same. The inference was clear: I must quack like a mother mallard in order to make the little ducks run after me. No sooner said than done. When, one Whit-Saturday, a brood of pure-bred young mallards was due to hatch, I put the eggs in the incubator, took the babies, as soon as they were dry, under my personal care, and quacked for them the mother's call-note in my best Mallardese. For hours on end I kept it up, for a half a day. The quacking was successful. The little ducks lifted their gaze confidently towards me, obviously had no fear of me this time, and as, still quacking, I drew

Goslings accept zoologist Lorenz as their mother.

slowly away from them, they also set themselves obediently in motion and scuttled after me in a tightly huddled group, just as ducklings follow their mother. My theory was indisputably proved. The freshly hatched ducklings have an inborn reaction to the call-note, but not to the optical picture of the mother. Anything that emits the right quack note will be considered as mother, whether it is a fat white Pekin duck or a still fatter man. However, the substituted object must not exceed a certain height. At the beginning of these experiments, I had sat myself down in the grass amongst the ducklings and, in order to make them follow me, had dragged myself, sitting, away from them. As soon, however, as I stood up and tried, in a standing posture, to lead them on, they gave up, peered searchingly on all sides, but not upwards towards me and it was not long before they began that penetrating piping of abandoned ducklings that we are accustomed simply to call "crying." They were unable to adapt themselves to the fact that their foster-mother had become so tall. So I was forced to move along, squatting low, if I wished them to follow me. This was not very comfortable; still less comfortable was the fact that the mallard mother quacks unintermittently. If I ceased for even the space of half a minute from my melodious "Quahg, gegegegeg, Quahg, gegegegeg," the necks of the ducklings became longer and longer corresponding exactly to "long faces" in human children—and did I then not immediately recommence quacking, the shrill weeping began anew. As soon as I was silent, they seemed to think that I had died, or perhaps that I loved them no more: cause enough for crying! The ducklings, in contrast to the greylag goslings, were most demanding and tiring charges, for, imagine a two-hour

walk with such children, all the time squatting low and quacking without interruption! In the interests of science I submitted myself literally for hours on end to this ordeal. So it came about, on a certain Whit-Sunday, that, in company with my ducklings, I was wandering about, squatting and quacking, in a May-green meadow at the upper part of our garden. I was congratulating myself on the obedience and exactitude with which my ducklings came waddling after me, when I suddenly looked up and saw the garden fence framed by a row of dead-white faces: a group of tourists was standing at the fence and staring horrified in my direction. Forgivable! For all they could see was a big man with a beard dragging himself, crouching, round the meadow, in figures of eight, glancing constantly over his shoulder and quacking—but the ducklings, the all-revealing and all-explaining ducklings were hidden in the tall spring grass from the view of the astonished crowd.

Lorenz leads a flock of goslings.

A Rich Array of Plumages

The extraordinary variety of markings displayed by ducks is readily apparent in the gallery of birds pictured on these pages. In the top row, the North American ruddy duck is a small bird with legs placed so far back on its body that it waddles clumsily on land, swims with its long, stiff tail feathers upright and lays the largest egg, in relation to its size, of any duck; the falcated teal, a swift-flying bird of eastern Asia, is fairly solitary except during migration.

In the middle row, the baldpate, or American widgeon, is a freshwater dweller that feeds almost exclusively on vegetable matter; the ringed teal is a native of South America and one of the more delicate of the waterfowl; the Radjah shelduck belongs to a quarrelsome family in which males fight as part of their courtship display, and the female se-lects the victor as her mate; the northern pintail is found in great abundance over most of the northern hemisphere.

In the bottom row, the pink-eared duck of Australia has a shovel-shaped bill with unique flapped appendages on either side that are capable of sifting the tiniest bits of algae from the water; the red-crested pochard, a gregarious, freshwater-loving bird, often travels in huge flocks and is found from southern Europe to Asia and Africa; the scaup is a hardy duck that inhabits large bodies of fresh water until winter, when it migrates to salt water (the scaup is said to be able to dive to depths of 20 feet in search of food); the Barrow's goldeneye, whose wings make a distinctive noise as it flies, nests in northwestern North America and southwestern Greenland and Iceland.

Baldpate

Ringed teal

Pink-eared duck

Red-crested pochard

Ruddy duck

Falcated teal

Radjah shelduck

Northern pintail

Scaup

Barrow's goldeneye

Hottentot Teals and Mergansers

The mergansers (opposite) exist mainly on a diet of fish. Their long, narrow bills, with their serrated edges, are especially well suited for catching and holding prey. The birds are also excellent divers, able to swim and plunge immediately after being hatched. Mergansers undergo an incubation period of 25 to 32 days and produce eight to 10 hatchlings. Although there are many mergansers that breed on fresh water, others spend most of their time in coastal areas. Sportsmen refer to them contemptuously as "trash ducks" and dislike them because, fortunately for the mergansers, their fish diet gives their meat an unappetizing flavor. A distant relative is the hottentot teal (above), one of the smaller ducks and probably the family's most accomplished flier.

Mergansers, such as the female American (left) and the hooded (below), are among the quieter birds, having only a few calls. Nearly all of them live in the cold or temperate parts of the northern hemisphere. The hooded merganser prefers to build its nest either in the hollow of a tree or on a cliff's ledge.

Geese and Swans

Few sights can compare with an echelon of swans on the wing. The great birds cruise the air with a matchless blend of elegance and power. They have been clocked at speeds of 40 to 50 miles per hour, and one, a whistler, collided with an airplane at an altitude of 6,000 feet at such a high speed that the plane was forced into a crash landing.

When they swim, swans are no less stately, and it is understandable that, for centuries, men have esteemed them as symbols of purity and nobility. More than 600 years ago the mute swan was designated the British royal bird; today some 18,000 swans belong to the Crown. Man's esteem is not reciprocated: Swans will attack any human who intrudes on their nesting territory. Belligerent, ill-tempered territorialists, they will not tolerate other swans, excepting their mates and young, and the general rule is for one pair of swans to occupy the same pond or stretch of stream for their 30- to 40-year life-span.

In ancient times swans were said to possess remarkable musical powers and to sing hauntingly at the hour of their death, a myth that has been perpetuated by poets and composers for centuries. Swans do not make any special sound, musical or otherwise, before they die, and the so-called mute swans are not really voiceless. Swans frequently hiss, grunt or, when they are caring for their young cygnets, even bark like dogs. And, although most swans are white, symbolizing purity in the eyes of poets and mythmakers, there are black swans in Australia and black-necked members of the family in South America.

Man's admiration for the great birds has not prevented the wholesale slaughter of swans for their flesh—a highly regarded table delicacy until recent times—and for their downy swanskins. Former kings of Denmark organized huge swan hunts during the molting seasons, when the birds lost their longer wing feathers and, unable to fly, were at the mercy of the royal hunters. In North America, swanskin hunters brought the trumpeter swan, the largest of all waterfowl, to the verge of extinction: By 1933 only 66 were counted in the United States. Since then, thanks to rigid protection laws and the creation of the Red Rock Lakes Wildlife Refuge in Montana, the trumpeters have made a remarkably strong comeback and as of 1971 numbered some 5,000 pairs. Young trumpeters usually pair at the age of three, almost always for life, and two years later, after an impressive courtship display, they begin mating. Their nests are large, nearly five feet across, and the three to

seven eggs the female, or pen, lays take approximately five weeks to incubate and hatch. The male, or cob, assists in protecting the young, and at the age of two months the baby swans, or cygnets, begin to fly. By October the entire family is ready to migrate together, a journey that may take them from Alaska or Canada south to Nevada, Montana and South Dakota. Normally aquatic feeders, often upending like ducks, trumpeters also graze on land for grasses and other vegetable matter, like geese. When threatened with capture and unable to fly, they may dive underwater, like ducks. When asleep they curve their long neck (swans have some 22 to 25 vertebrae, geese fewer than 20) back toward their tail, tucking the tip of their bill snugly under one wing.

The world's 14 species of geese are a link between the larger swans and smaller ducks in the family Anatidae. Like swans, geese have long necks and legs and regularly graze on land. The sexes are not differentiated by color. They also molt only once a year, losing their feathers and replacing them gradually, temporarily losing their powers of flight as ducks and swans do. Like ducks, they upend when feeding on the water, and their windpipes are simple and not convoluted as are those of some swans.

All geese are highly territorial, especially at breeding time, and may suddenly attack invaders with utter fearlessness. More than 100 years ago Audubon wrote about a gander that, when he approached its nest, attacked him with such fury that he thought his arm was broken.

Strong, dogged fliers, Canada geese are remarkable migrators. Cruising in trailing skeins or V formations at speeds better than 40 miles per hour, they may winter on the East Coast or in California or 4,000 miles away in Mexico. The champion aerialist in the family, having more wing area than any other goose, is the bar-headed goose, so called for the two bar markings across its head. A native of central Asia, this great bird has been spotted crossing Himalayan passes at altitudes of 20,000 feet. Bar-headed geese normally nest in the open in dense colonies at altitudes up to 16,000 feet. Most common in Europe and Asia is the graylag goose, the ancestor of all domestic strains except those found in China. Its diet consists generally of grasses, tubers, acorns and grain. In certain parts of Europe it is force-fed large quantities of grain, which grossly enlarges its liver, from which paté de fois gras is produced.

114

Mute swan

A Skein of Snow Geese

Heralding their arrival with loud honking calls, hundreds of snow geese (left) cloud the sky in a southward swing from their breeding sites on the Arctic shores of Alaska and Canada to their wintering grounds, which range as far south as the Gulf of Mexico—a journey of almost 3,000 miles. There are two species, the lesser snow goose, one of the most common of the North American geese, and the heavier-bodied but less numerous greater snow goose. Both species bear a remarkable resemblance to swans but are distinguished by their black wing tips and shorter necks. Unlike the snow goose, the noisy and quarrelsome Egyptian goose (below) is a solitary traveler. The only time these inhabitants of central and southern Africa gather together is during their periodic molt, and even then the group numbers only a handful of individuals.

Flying Wedges

When they are traveling for only a few miles, geese, like all waterfowl, have relatively indistinct flying formations. But when they move over long distances to their wintering grounds, like the migrating Canada geese (above) or snow geese (right), the birds fly in well-defined V's as neat and crisp as military chevrons. This arrangement gives each bird room to flap its wings, which can span up to five feet, plus an almost unobstructed view. Generally led by a female, the birds persist in their flight day and night, stopping only for brief spells when they are hungry or tired. During these stopovers several birds stand guard as the others feed. A warning call from one of the sentinels is all its takes to bring the entire flock to full alert, poised for instant takeoff should danger present itself.

The Courtship of the Canada Goose *by John James Audubon*

Audubon's The Birds of America, *with its magnificent hand-colored plates, and the companion text,* Ornithological Biographies, *both published in 1839, were landmark studies of bird life and brought the artist-ornithologist immediate world acclaim and financial success. It took Audubon 12 years (1827–1839) to produce the life-size portraits and the text. Reprinted here is his description of the courtship of the Canada goose and his magnificent portrait of the great bird.*

It is extremely amusing to witness the courtship of the Canada Goose in all its stages; and let me assure you, reader, that although a Gander does not strut before his beloved with the pomposity of a Turkey, or the grace of a Dove, his ways are quite as agreeable to the female of his choice. I can imagine before me one who has just accomplished the defeat of another male after a struggle of half an hour or more. He advances gallantly towards the object of contention, his head scarcely raised an inch from the ground, his bill open to its full stretch, his fleshy tongue elevated, his eyes darting fiery glances, and as he moves he hisses loudly, while the emotion which he experiences causes his quills to shake, and his feathers to rustle. Now he is close to her who in his eyes is all loveliness; his neck bending gracefully in all directions, passes all round her, and occasionally touches her body; and as she congratulates him on his victory, and acknowledges his affection, they move their necks in a hundred curious ways. At this moment fierce jealousy urges the defeated gander to renew his efforts to obtain his love; he advances apace, his eyes glowing with the fire of rage; he shakes his broad wings, ruffles up his whole plumage, and as he rushes on the foe, hisses with the intensity of anger. The whole flock seems to stand amazed, and opening up a space, the birds gather round to view the combat. The bold bird who has been caressing his mate, scarcely deigns to take notice of his foe, but seems to send a scornful glance towards him. He of the mortified feelings, however, raises his body, half opens his sinewy wings, and with a powerful blow, sends forth his defiance. The affront cannot be borne in the presence of so large a company, nor indeed is there much dispositon to bear it in any circumstances; the blow is returned with vigour, the aggressor reels for a moment, but he soon recovers, and now the combat rages. Were the weapons more deadly, feats of chivalry would now be performed; as it is, thrust and blow succeed each other like the strokes of hammers driven by sturdy forgers. But now, the mated gander has caught hold of his antagonist's head with his bill; no bull-dog could cling faster to his victim; he squeezes him with all the energy of rage, lashes him with his powerful wings, and at length drives him away, spreads out his pinions, runs with joy to his mate, and fills the air with cries of exultation.

Family Flotilla

Swans are readily distinguished from geese by their elegant necks, which are often longer than their bodies. The Eurasian mute swan (below), with its cygnet nestled snugly among its snowy feathers, and its close relative, the Australian black swan (opposite, below), usually hold their necks in a characteristic, flowing S-curve, with their beaks pointed downward. The North American trumpeter swan (opposite, above), the largest and rarest of the swans, generally keeps its long neck erect and its bill pointed straight ahead. By changes in their posture the gregarious swans communicate to other members of their flock when they are about to fly—an important signal, for larger-bodied birds need considerable takeoff space. Thus the flight of a mute or black swan is heralded when the bird raises its neck, smoothes its plumage and faces into the wind. The trumpeter swan, on the other hand, announces its departure (see overleaf) by shaking its head rapidly from side to side and emitting its magnificent clarion call.

Once they mate, swans remain together for life. Both partners share in building their nest, defending and incubating their eggs and caring for their young. While swimming, the mute swan (opposite) often carries its young on its back, especially during the first week after hatching, when the cygnet is weak and vulnerable. All young waterfowl, such as the black swan chick and its parent at left, can swim and feed themselves just after hatching, and during their first few months they live on water insects and aquatic vegetation. Swan families, like the trumpeter swans above, stay together for about nine months until the start of the next breeding season, when the young are forced to leave and spend the summer with other immature and nonbreeding birds.

123

Credits

Bibliography

NOTE: Asterisk at the left means that a paperback volume is also listed in *Books in Print*.

Alexander, Wilfred B., *Birds of the Ocean*. Putnam, 1963.

Audubon, John James, *Ornithological Biography*. Edinburgh, 1831–1839.

Audubon, Marie, *Audubon and his Journals*. Dover, 1960.

Austin, Oliver, *Birds of the World*. Golden Press, 1961.

Beebe, William, *Nonsuch: Land of Water*. National Travel Club, 1932.

*Bent, Arthur Cleveland, *Life Histories of North American Shore Birds*. Peter Smith, 1962.

Brown, Leslie, and Amadon, Dean. *Eagles, Hawks and Falcons of the World* (2 vols.). McGraw-Hill, 1968.

Bruun, Bertel, *Birds of Europe*. McGraw-Hill, 1971.

Delacour, J., *The Waterfowl of the World* (4 vols.). Arco, 1974.

Fisher, James, and Lockley, R. M., *Seabirds*. Houghton Mifflin, 1954.

———, and Peterson, Roger Tory, *The World of Birds*. MacDonald, 1964.

Gooders, John, *The Great Book of Birds*. Dial Press, 1975.

Grzimek, Bernhard, *Grzimek's Animal Life Encyclopedia* (vols. 7 and 8). Van Nostrand Reinhold, 1972.

*Hochbaum, H. A., *Travels and Traditions of Waterfowl*. University of Minnesota Press, 1956.

Huxley, Julian, *Essays of a Biologist*. Chatto and Windus, 1926.

Johnsgard, Paul A., *Waterfowl*. University of Nebraska Press, 1968.

Kortright, F. H., *Ducks, Geese and Swans of North America*. Stackpole, 1942.

Murphy, R. C., *Oceanic Birds of South America* (2 vols.). American Museum of Natural History, 1936.

Peterson, Roger Tory, *The Bird Watchers Anthology*. Harcourt, Brace, 1957.

———, and the editors of Time-Life Books, *The Birds*. Time-Life Books, 1963.

*Saunders, David, *Sea Birds*. Grosset & Dunlap, 1973.

Scott, Peter, and the Wildlife Trust, *The Swans*. Houghton Mifflin, 1972.

*Short, Lester L., *Birds of the World*. Ridge Press, 1975.

Stokes, Ted, *Birds of the Atlantic Ocean*. Country Life Books, 1968.

Stonehouse, B., *Penguins*. Arthur Baker, 1968.

Stout, Gardner (ed.), text by Peter Matthiessen, *Shorebirds of North America*. Viking, 1967.

*Tinbergen, Nikolaas, *The Herring Gull's World*. Doubleday, 1961.

Vaucher, Charles, *Sea Birds*. Oliver and Boyd, 1960.

Watson, George C., *Sea Birds of the Tropical Atlantic Ocean*. Random House, 1966.

Welty, J. C., *The Life of Birds*. Knopf, 1963.

Wetmore, Alexander (ed.), *Water, Prey and Game Birds of North America*. National Geographic Society, 1965.

Williamson, Kenneth, *The Atlantic Island*. Routledge and Kegan Paul, 1970.

Wilson, Edward, *Birds of the Antarctic*. Humanities Press, 1967.

Index